Myra
75

"Shozan Jack Haubner has the rare, the enviable, gift of being sneakily wise, un-pious, liberating, and 1000 percent himself, all while not seeming to take too much too seriously. I've grown drunk on his pieces—teetotaler though I am—for years now, and keep foisting his exhilaratingly honest, unique, fearless, and sometimes scurrilous essays on everyone I care about. The man sounds as if he knows Zen practice so deeply that he's come out at the other end, full of candor, fresh air, and the constant slaps of humor that are all that can wake some of us up as we fall into our ruts and fantasies of happy endings. Reading *Single White Monk*, I had to keep a notebook by my side to catch the startling truths—about death, about ego, about suffering—that kept flashing out from its riotous pages."

—PICO IYER, author of *Video Night in Kathmandu* and *Sun After Dark*

"A lot of books, movies, and TV shows present pretty fantasies of the lives of Zen monks. Those are cute, but I doubt they do anything but fill people's heads with unrealistic dreams. Shozan writes about what it's really like, which is way more valuable."

—BRAD WARNER, author of *Hardcore Zen* and *Don't Be a Jerk: And Other Practical Advice from Dōgen, Japan's Greatest Zen Master*

Also by Shozan Jack Haubner

Zen Confidential: Confessions of a Wayward Monk

Single White Monk

TALES OF DEATH,
FAILURE, AND BAD SEX
(ALTHOUGH NOT NECESSARILY IN THAT ORDER)

Shozan Jack Haubner

SHAMBHALA
Boulder
2017

Shambhala Publications, Inc.
4720 Walnut Street
Boulder, Colorado 80301
www.shambhala.com

9 8 7 6 5 4 3 2 1

First Edition
Printed in the United States of America

⊗ This edition is printed on acid-free paper that meets the
American National Standards Institute z39.48 Standard.
♻ This book is printed on 30% postconsumer recycled paper.
For more information please visit www.shambhala.com.
Distributed in the United States by Penguin Random House LLC
and in Canada by Random House of Canada Ltd

LIBRARY OF CONGRESS CATALOGING-IN-PUBLICATION DATA
Names: Haubner, Shozan Jack, author.
Title: Single white monk: tales of death, failure, and bad sex
(although not necessarily in that order) / Shozan Jack Haubner.
Description: First Edition. | Boulder: Shambhala, 2017.
Identifiers: LCCN 2016055502 | ISBN 9781611803631 (pbk.: alk. paper)
Subjects: LCSH: Haubner, Shozan Jack. | Zen Buddhists—United States—
Biography. | Buddhist monks—United States—Biography.
Classification: LCC BQ962.A85 A3 2017 | DDC 294.3/927092 [B]—dc23
LC record available at https://lccn.loc.gov/2016055502

For Roshi, Sokai, and Jikan
The Zen master, saint, and artist

And for the Sangha
You know who you are

Contents

Eating the Shadow:
An Introduction

The truth has a way of getting out, whether we like it or not. Usually, though, it comes out all wrong. Truth telling is not a straightforward or simple process. It always requires a birth, and births are messy. You cannot recall what happened—you recreate it.

This book is a collision of journal entries, reportage, creative misremembering, and fictional devices including compressed and invented events and characters (I rarely use real names except for pets). I call this genre *personal mythology*. The stories told are not a record of objective reality. They are the fever dream of a man wrestling with his memory, his teacher, his lovers, his peers, and himself. Let's just say the whole book was inspired by a true story—as if there were such a thing.

I have been searching for a true story my whole life. Writing and spirituality have always been intimately connected for me. I began writing in earnest my junior year of high school when I had what some might call a spiritual opening, though for me it was more like a taste of unfiltered reality. I was driving my beat-up station wagon down the 94 Freeway just outside of Milwaukee. It was a humid, starry night. In case you're wondering, I'd spilled some manure in the back seat a few months earlier that thunderstorms then soaked through a broken window. Now tiny green sprouts were growing up from the torn seat cushions, because that's how I roll.

I felt awesome. Earlier in the evening I'd danced with a pretty senior (who had a slight mustache) in a friend's big blue gazebo. Something was very right with the world, and it was getting righter and righter, yet there was nothing special about the moment. I simply looked out the passenger window as the giant outdoor movie theater whizzed by. Then something completely shifted. It was like the bottom of my mind dropped out. This moment changed the course of my life (I was going to write TV commercials), yet the texture and feel of the opening itself is lost to me. I came back to myself instantly, and all that was left was a question. The opening had no content. The question, however, was a tiny jewel. I turned it over and over inside me for decades.

Why is there something rather than nothing? Nothingness makes so much more sense.

In Zen, we learn that these two—indeed, *all*—opposites depend on each other. My Zen teacher, the Roshi, taught that you could call the world outside of you, the world of distinctions, of bright and shiny things, Father. And you could call the world inside of you, the rich, embryonic inner darkness, Mother. Sometimes the infinity of things outside of you penetrates through the sense gates—sight, sound, smell, touch, taste—and dissolves within the inner darkness, the fathomless psyche. Other times the formlessness within expands outward, embracing the world of form through your actions. From either outside coming in, or inside going out, a new thought or feeling arises and your sense of self is born in a process analogous to a baby crowning through a mother's hips. In this way a new self is being conceived, arising, and passing away every instant—sometimes initiating, sometimes receiving, but always appearing and disappearing at the meeting point between something and nothing.

Roshi called this True Love. He described it over and over, but it took years before I was able to live his words with my whole body. After moving to the monastery to study Zen full time I eventually became the head monk. Every morning we would gather at the work-bell and get our assignments from the work officer. Then I would turn around and head up the stone stairs for the office without thinking twice about it. One day I turned to head up the stairs when I realized that I was going from one conversation, the one behind me, to another, the one waiting for me in the office. I'd been doing this my entire life: shaking loose the moment behind me while anticipating the one ahead. One thing I had never done was simply walk up a flight of stairs.

To cultivate the mind of meditation is to stop looking forward to or dreading the next moment, and to stop reliving or regretting the past moment, and to start living in this one. The present comes fully equipped. To pursue happiness usually means rushing right past it.

Suddenly I experienced the miracle of locomotion, the way legs do their thing, carrying me like two faithful, marching animals; the way the space before me manifests a split second later as myself. It felt like I was scaling a flight of stairs for the very first time, and in a way I was. Once you discover your own legs and the ground beneath your feet, the path becomes clear. It is, quite simply, wherever you choose to go.

But in order for something new to be born into, and as, the next moment, something old must first die—this too is True Love. "You must completely die with me," Roshi would say during our private meetings. Then he would reach out and hug me. The world stopped when I was in this old man's soft arms.

Death through love . . . I had always thought of death as the moment where you *lose* everything, but Roshi taught me that death is where you *merge* with everything—where boundaries fade and fail. The great death that Zen masters speak of is analogous to Christ's death on the cross. It is a death so complete that it passes through or reverses itself and manifests as resurrection. It is the death spoken of by Joseph Campbell when he claims that in the dire apogee of the Hero's Journey, the universal template for storytelling, the protagonist must perish unto her old self and be reborn anew.

Unfortunately, a fear of death is coded into our culture. We are a nation of winners, and death is the ultimate loss. We don't talk about it much. We don't sit with our freshly deceased, pray with them, or feel their death all around and inside of us. We don't have many rituals around death—we have laws. If, as a culture, we are terrified and in denial of death, what does that say about our way of life?

Death is part of us. We need to own that. A nurse once told me that patients always die exactly as they lived. If they were feckless, courageous, or grouchy in life, so will they be on their deathbeds. In this way, our final moments are a reckoning—they speak to how we lived. When I was twenty, I had a death wish that coincided with my passion for skydiving. On my tenth jump I decided to press my luck. The instant you leap from an airplane your foot instinctively reaches for the earth beneath it. Then it floats back up and your body realizes it is 10,000 feet above ground. You are flying . . . flying . . . falling. I watched my altimeter drop below 2,500 feet—I did not pull my ripcord at this, the required, point. I closed my eyes and waited . . . then I pulled it when I was ready.

The low pull meant I was far away from the landing zone. I steered my parachute handily, but I couldn't avoid a power line right by the home base. As I soared over the wires I had to lift my feet, barely missing them. My jumpmaster went ballistic and grounded me for a month. About a year later he went on a tandem jump with a newlywed. His parachute malfunctioned and they both pounded into a golf course. They were reduced, as my father who was there, put it, "to hamburger."

Back then I figured that my instructor was afraid of death, so death smelled his fear and found him. I've come to believe that a youth who doesn't fear death is a fool who doesn't understand life. I loved the idea of heroically crashing into power lines and having relatives speak at my funeral of my daring personality. What truly terrified me, I realize now, was the thought of surviving the accident and lying paralyzed on a hospital bed. That's the difference between the young man I was and the middle-aged man I've become. Where I once risked death to avoid facing the hard facts of life, I now see those same hard facts as instances where death and life intersect, and neither really has the upper hand. This is the realm of sickness, anguish, failure, poverty, and really bad sex—where most of us live. Or at least where I was living when I wrote this book.

The night I e-mailed the final draft of my first book to the publishers, Roshi got violently ill. He would never formally teach again. This marked the beginning of a dark time in our community, which intensified unbearably when a sex scandal involving Roshi broke. As one of his two primary caretakers, and the head monk at his main monastery, I was at the heart of this darkness, and the darkness became mine. (That's how darkness works. It's contagious.) Two years after the scandal, when Roshi was walking, as the Japanese say, his one hundred eighth year, he died. By then most of his senior students had become senior citizens. Pretty soon they started passing away too. We lost a long list of practitioners (and pets) in a short period of time.

One night I was in the zendo trying to meditate when I broke down crying. There was no one there. It was just me and my empty zendo. I had recently given a dharma talk where I'd told the students, "The problem is always that you want things to be other than the way they are." So I asked myself: What is it that you cannot accept about your life? And it came to me then: You don't want to die. I fought with myself on this: I'm not afraid of death, I've never been afraid of death. Then I realized: No, that's not what I said, I said, *you don't want to die.*

My big mistake was thinking that life is the opposite of death. The opposite of death is not life, it is birth. Life, rather, is equal parts birth and death, with the first half of life favoring growth, possibility, action, and the second half giving way to reflection, frailty, annihilation. I wasn't afraid of being dead, I was afraid of the way death slowly takes over your life: in a silent moment when you know you will never fall in love again; when you realize you've been faking it at your job for decades and the younger generation is not fooled. Sitting in the zendo that night, I realized I was now heading inexorably toward death. I was crying the tears of a middle-aged man, tears I must have known were coming back when I had my skydiving death wish and I wanted to go out when I was full of potential and hope instead of regret and despair.

This is the great death that awaits all of us in middle age—the death of our illusions, of the fantasy that we can get life completely right, that our team will finally win. If we knew these things when we were young, we would all probably nosedive into our own personal power lines. I have always felt that the one trade-off for getting old is becoming wise. Wisdom, like any ecosystem, is the marriage of uncountable factors over a long period of time. It is our most precious resource, for the wise heart unites within itself the conflicts that divide the world around it. It is here that my writing and Zen paths converge.

In writing, you take a thesis and get it going, or you conjure a protagonist and put her on a path. Then you throw up an obstacle—an antithesis or villain. Through their relationship (war is weak intimacy, as the saying goes) an answer is born, a *synthesis*. This synthesis is the manifestation of True Love, the marriage of opposing forces. In these pages, I am both protagonist and antagonist. I like to be the center of attention. Put another way, I'm self-centered, a self that I am trying to kill off in every scene.

Every book should start with an apology for itself. Writing creates conflict to tell a story. The whole project implies that man must suffer to grow. This sends the wrong message. We learn from direct experience through Zen practice that peace is available right here and now if only we can let go of our stories, conflicts, and dramas. No book is necessary, least of all this one. Don't be fooled. The whole thing is just me trying to convince both of us that I am solid, real, that I matter, that I will go on mattering after I die. Do you really need to be a part of this? It's the same old thing. Some guy trying to make a name for himself. As a nun told me, "Just because you know how to use words, doesn't mean you tell the truth."

You cannot tell the truth. Truth is in the silence between words, the opening before the great question, the place where lovers meet, die into each other, birth something new. It's just about anywhere but a book.

This book took me five years to write, and I was never not living inside of it and the sublime horrors that gave rise to it—the deaths, always the deaths. Without writing, I fear that I too would have been a casualty. You have to put your energy somewhere, otherwise it doubles back on you and you drive your Subaru off the mountain, subconsciously create a cancer for yourself, or perish in stages, one drink at a time. I am so sorry, but I had to write it. Art is a socially acceptable form of inflicting your suffering on others. And this is not even art!

But enough of this. It's disingenuous. There is a right way and a wrong way to die while living, and I have tried to do it right, consciously—on the page, at least. I'll own that. In every chapter I'm trying to shed skin, get down to the bone, let you contemplate death in its many forms with me, like the Vedantic sadhus who meditate in charnel grounds beside smoldering corpses. Let's look at this thing together. Here we are, alive, the universe seeing itself through our eyes. We have but a few precious years left. Pay attention to all of it, the good and the bad. Perhaps especially the bad. Because in reflecting on it, we are drawn by contrast to the good. But more importantly, we discover how good and bad can exist together in one world.

You taught me that, Roshi.

At the height of the sex scandal, the filmmaker shooting a documentary about Roshi asked him about the allegations against him. Her question amounted to: How can both dark and light exist within the heart of one man? He looked past the cameras, lights, bundles of cords and equipment and found my eyes across the room, where I was trying to hide from him.

"One cosmos. Both good and bad, right and wrong, Hitler and Roosevelt together in this one cosmos. How?" he said.

That's the question, the *koan*, at the heart of this book.

Both good and evil, truth and lies, birth and death, something and nothing, together in this one cosmos, this one life, this one heart—your heart.

How?

PART ONE

Middle-Aged Middle Manager of the Middle Way

1

Middle-Way Manager

At night I lie in bed, unable to sleep. Worst-case scenarios run through my head—and then I remember that they're not worst-case scenarios at all. I'm living them. Roshi died (he died four times, actually—more on that later), our community has torn itself apart in his absence, and I'm forty, single, and still not totally sure what I want to do with my life.

Plus I have the prostate of a seventy-year-old man, which is not as fun as it sounds. At night I pee in an old plastic mozzarella cheese bucket I keep by the side of the bed, because I pee a lot and the bathroom is too far down the hall. I mean, it's not in another zip code or something, but the stone hallway tile is really hard and cold, and anyway, don't judge me. One man's sad little habit is another man's life hack.

Not long ago I left the monastery. Now I live at and manage the head temple in LA that Roshi founded fifty years ago. The halls are haunted by his absence. The place is full of ghosts. At night they all seem to take up residence in my room—in my *head*. I can't stop worrying. Mostly I worry about how the temple will survive on my limited charisma and Cracker Jack insights. Who will want to come study with me? Is it my job to be spiritually impressive, to draw in new students, or is this just ego?

I never wanted to make a career out of Zen. I simply wanted to find a way to live. Making a living at being wise seems to come so naturally to some people. They write a few books, smile from a few lifestyle-magazine covers, and suddenly they're filling auditoriums. Bastards. I belong to a different class. Not a spiritual superstar, but not a freshman practitioner either. Not enlightened, but I can help a rookie upgrade her practice. I deal in small volumes of local dharma.

I'm a middle-way manager.

After my *suiji-shiki*, or priest/teacher ordination ceremony, they put me in the temple tearoom as a kind of dharma show pony. There I stood, in thirty pounds of hand-sewn garments, trying to make sense of my new red-and-gold fan, when a Japanese woman, about fifty years of age, approached me, went down on her knees before me, and began bowing and saying, "Shozan-san! Thank you! Thank you!" "Okay," I said, bowing my head, "Yes, thank *you*." "Thank you! Thank you, Shozan-san!" She stayed down there an awfully long time and I began to go red in the face. "Okay, yes, thank you, too. Okay . . ." "*Thank you, Shozan-san!*"

There were tears in people's eyes. Everyone looked so in love with their idea of me just then. And who was I to argue? Much of your job as a new Zen priest involves pretending that you actually are the kind of person that people keep mistaking you for. You are constantly walking the thin line between growing into your new role and faking the part.

That being said, whatever you do, don't try to hide your weaknesses. This is the spiritual equivalent of combing the hair down by your ears up over the shiny bald spot on the top of your head. No one's fooled. The only thing worse than trying to look younger than you are is trying to look wiser than you are.

Of course you can't win, because once you're open about your flaws, students judge you every bit as harshly as you used to judge the teachers in your own life. They even compare you to your own spiritual heroes, often with a look on their face as though they've eaten a bad piece of fish, and suddenly you realize that those deep souls who inspired you are somehow now your competitors—and you go from admiring to envying them.

Envy is born from insecurity. We often think that insecurity comes from a weak ego, but in my experience insecurity is the result of an inflexible ego that has mistaken itself as the center of the universe, which keeps contradicting it on this key point. Whatever its origin, envy is not the proper response to spiritual decency in others. Yet there it was, rising up in me just the other night after I peed in my cheese bucket. I lay back down and started thinking about how many truly extraordinary Buddhist teachers there are in this world, and how lucky I am that they all live so far away. I mean, how could I compete for students with the Dalai Lama?

I tried to puff myself up by thinking about the book I wrote and its dozens of fans. Then I remembered who it is shelved next to at Barnes & Noble. Thich Nhat something or another. There are about five hundred titles in the Eastern religions section, and at least a thousand of them are written by him. Who writes this many books? How does he do it? They just fall out of him, one after another, sometimes two at a time, like children from the Octomom.

I went on in this vein until the sun started to rise and I had to pee again. I stumbled out of bed and stepped right into my bucket of urine—at which point I utterly freaked out. I thought I'd fallen into a frigid pool of death. I screamed and kicked my foot, and the pee bucket shot right through my paper shoji screen and across the room, where it hit the wall and landed with a thud.

I cleaned up my mess, cursed creatively, crawled back in bed, and lay there like the middle-aged ersatz Eckhart Tolle I am. No way I was falling asleep now. I replayed the pee-bucket incident again and again in my head, audibly groaning each time. The worst person to be embarrassed in front of is yourself, because out of everyone you know you're probably the least willing to forget any of the stupid things that you do.

Humility, however, brings clarity. Sometimes you're just too busy thinking about yourself to really see yourself clearly. That's when life puts a banana peel—or a pee bucket—in your path. That morning I clearly saw just how heavy I had grown with the burden of trying to be someone who I am not. I needed to go back to the core of Zen practice: doing simple things completely, not trying to do big things for a large audience. I'm a monk, not Tony Robbins. If people get something out of practicing with me, great. But I can't carry anyone into the zendo with me, either through charisma, insight, or marketing. That's just not what this path is about. People have to bring themselves to the practice. And when they do, I'm there to practice with them.

My job as a middle-aged middle manager of the middle way is the same as that of any lay practitioner, right on up to the most enlightened being on earth: we all must commit wholeheartedly, moment after moment, to the life we have, instead of fantasizing about a different life while putting down or envying those who are supposedly living it. When I start feeling jealous of others, it's a warning sign that I've become a little bit too entranced by some idea of myself and have lost touch with the reality of my life. Someone else seems to better represent this idea of myself than I do, and suddenly I want his life instead of my own.

Zen practice, however, teaches you to completely be yourself—if you don't, who will? Someone's got to hold down your corner of the universe, and no one else is qualified. If you are not fully present in your life, there will be an absence in the world where you should be. That absence won't be big or small, it will be the exact same size as your presence—perfectly you-sized.

The first thing I teach new Zen students is to follow their breath, and I finally found peace that morning when I followed mine. I drifted to sleep with images of nobodies from all over the world in my head. Billions of us. Serving coffee, writing parking tickets, ringing those bells at Trader Joe's, breastfeeding children, saving lives. Remove us from the workplace, from schools, from the church and home and hospitals, and the life will be choked out of these institutions in a few sharp gasps. We are invisible, ubiquitous, and essential—like the very air we breathe.

If you feel insignificant, *and* you take yourself too seriously, you're never going to get any sleep at night. So relax—the best way to realize no-self is to laugh at yourself. After the Japanese woman finally got up from her knees that day in the tearoom, a tall, skinny monk friend of mine took her place before me. Everything about him is lanky, even his long, narrow teeth. He saw my expression and growled. "Don't forget the most important thing about being a Zen priest—*wear your responsibilities lightly!*"

It was one of those rare moments where someone says something that you didn't know you needed to hear, and it makes all the difference. A well-put spiritual phrase usually happens like this, by accident or chance, in response to some particular need. Genuine teaching arises in small moments, person to person. At least that's always how it's been for me. When you're fully present in your life, the teachings have a way of finding you—and when you're not, a bucket of piss becomes the Buddha and wakes you up.

2

Dirt Monkey

My first two Zen teachers were, in this order, failure and my father. And the very first thing I failed at was being physically big. This wasn't my fault, of course, but kids always feel directly responsible for how they look. And how I looked was wimpy.

To wit, a Christmas photo survives from my youth. My sister is wearing a camisole unitard and pointe shoes, and is managing a full-face power smile seemingly achieved with the help of invisible pulleys stretching her cheeks in opposite directions. And who's that little sprite to her right? Me, at age six, in cowboy couture. It's as though our gifts got switched and we're wearing each other's outfits. She is beefy and dense, her round flushed face a cannonball of concentration as she struggles to put some distance between that fleshy foot of hers and the ground. I, on the other hand, am lithe, graceful, with Kermit the Frog gams that would look adorable jutting out from under a frilly pink tutu. But alas, in my tight, flared leather chaps and matching vest sans shirt underneath, with those bulging brown eyes and that permanently terrified grin, I resemble an underage homoerotic Don Knotts.

Years passed. The seasons changed. My body weight did not. Eventually I sprouted a few perfunctory black hairs in the appropriate regions, but then puberty forgot all about me, leaving the task less than half done. I stayed pretty much the same size throughout middle school. My health-food-conscious mother augmented my diet with Malabar, a gooey gray protein supplement, which featured—right there, in the ingredients!—cow brain and spleen, but to no avail. I could have swallowed a truck tire and my metabolism would have shrugged and disintegrated it. "Spaz" was the peewee-soccer nickname I earned owing to an energy level incommensurate with my body size. If small, I made for a rather large target for bullies. When a boy-man of a goalie tipped over the port-a-potty where I was trying to hide from him, I decided to start pumping stones. Overnight I became a crazy little bug-eyed seventh grader in a spaghetti-string tank top, curling buckets of rocks in the basement and squeaking self-encouragements like an amped-up field mouse.

"One . . . more . . . rep!"

Every Friday night I would present my father with a tape measure from my grandmother's old sewing box. Once scrawny like me, Dad became a man of iron in his late teens with the same intensity of purpose that he pursued all his goals. Now he had sixteen-inch pipes and thick, striated jaw muscles from using his mouth to curl a free weight that was tied to a rope that he looped up over his lower jaw. ("Had to flesh out my face. I had cheeks like Ichabod Crane!")

"Can you measure me?" I tore off my Gold's Gym tank top and tremble-flexed. My whole body convulsed as I tried to swell that dainty little Ping-Pong ball of muscle.

Peering over his reading glasses, Dad circled the tape around my bicep, studying it carefully. "Ten and a half inches," he relayed.

And so I strained harder, clenching everything from my eye-teeth to my anus, the veins pitchforking across my forehead from underneath my mullet. It looked like I was peeing on an electric fence.

"Ten . . . and a half . . . inches," he confirmed, and I nearly collapsed under the sinking feeling that weighed on me my whole youth: I just didn't measure up. I was an inferior version of myself.

A good Catholic boy, I decided to petition my Maker with the hope that he might reconsider his decision to give me a girl's body with boy's genitals. My mother taught me that if you ask the Blessed Virgin Mary for anything, she will ask her son Jesus to ask God the Father to grant your wish. From what I had seen of family dynamics this was just complicated enough to be believable. I spent hours alone on my knees before my middle school's life-size Virgin Mary statue. I prayed for a wink from her painted eye, begged her to rustle her plaster robes, which tastefully concealed her shapely form.

I prayed for a miracle. I prayed to be big.

The Virgin stood frozen, inert, one chipped foot peeking out from under her azure robe, where it crushed, but never released, the skull of a tiny mutant Satan who resembled a brown and be-fanged Spanky from the *Little Rascals*. Unfortunately, the Holy Matron did not use her considerable pull to help me bulk up my pipes, and my arms remained pipe cleaners. I spent several shirtless hours a week flexing before the bathroom mirror, trying to will myself into a bigger state. But mirrors never lie. So I took the matter of my failed prayers to my own in-house religious complaints department. My mother was cubing hunks of venison with a massive silver blade before rippling kitchen window drapes. She turned to me and ran her hands, lacquered to the wrists in deer blood, across her white apron, leaving calligraphic bolts. Then she tightened her black hair in its bun, fixed me with her soft-brown eyes, which were perpetually liquid with confusion and love, those hallmarks of a nervous young mother, and she said . . .

I don't remember what she said. Her answer has been resigned to the dustbin of forgotten parental platitudes. My voice had begun to crack, and my manhood, formerly as smooth and tiny as a triple-A battery, now resembled a pinkish baby bird perpetually falling out of its nest. These developments coincided with the realization that my mother was no longer the go-to parent on matters weightier than curfews or allowance. I began to question her beliefs, which she'd so desperately tried to graft on to the nascent green shoots of my spiritual yearnings.

I also began to observe my father's religious inclinations, or lack thereof. Every Sunday he would take his place at the end of our pew, and like a junkie getting the nods, pass out. He made a great show of passing out, in fact. "Ah, Catholicism," he seemed to be saying, "you bring out the vegetative state in me." We began to fall asleep together during Mass: father and son, side by side, mouths open, bodies slumped—dreaming about being elsewhere, doing other things.

What Dad dreamed about was shooting guns. If he rejected Catholicism, his passion for rifles was religious. We spent long hours at the Daniel Boone Rifle Range. *Thump!* His shot would whack the hillside behind me. *Rrrrring* . . . I'd grab a rope and pull the target on its rollers down into the concrete trench where I was waiting to plug it with a cardboard marker and roll it back up.

Thump! Rrrrring. Hour after hour, as the hot wet summer air thrilled with the horny harmony of cicadas. It was achingly boring, and the best possible thing for me, anxious child that I was. It's good to see your father made solid by doing what he loves. It makes you feel solid too.

"Sight alignment is paramount," he explained late one afternoon, as the sun tipped its hat on the horizon. He hovered over me and tweaked my prone form by putting pressure on various parts of my body until they naturally moved into place, and then relaxing his hand. Posture, stillness, relaxation, focus: but most important when it came to hitting the mark was breathing.

"When you stop exhaling, just when you're about to breathe in, in that moment of repose, you sort of let the trigger almost pull itself," Dad said. (The second person to direct my attention to this "sweet spot" was a Vedantic meditation guru in LA some fifteen years later. In my mind's eye my father pokes his head through the window of the guru's *satsang* gazebo and announces, "He heard it from me first, Swami.")

This moment was everything—where you lost yourself in the act, which then somehow completed itself. Fathers have taught sons this lesson since the beginning of time: how to do things right, fully, with a complete heart, mastering a task only by first surrendering to it completely. I needed this. I did not need my mother's belief system. I needed a way of life. I needed to get lost in the rigors of release. I needed a religion that would snap me, and take me into manhood and something greater than myself.

One morning my freshman year in high school, as I hunched over my locker, a pair of hulking legs appeared behind me. I followed them up the torso of Todd Hunter, whose blue eyes hooked into my face like a pair of talons. There was a lot of him to take in, most of it muscle. Even his hair looked angry—bright red. With a surgical scar running the length of his chest, and a flair for charismatic violence, Todd was a legend. During a football game against the School for the Deaf, he took over the coach's halftime pep talk and vowed to put two of the opposing team's players in the hospital. He did just that. Two ambulances came before the end of the game and loaded up two small, stunned running backs as they released frightened groans.

I saw that Todd was engrossed in the pictures of a bodybuilder I'd taped to my locker door. In my zeal to become big, I'd become obsessed with Lee Haney, eight-time Mr. Olympia. He had cinder blocks of rippling flesh that looked like the sort of thing a mad geneticist might grow in a huge tube. His oiled black face was shrouded in a net of veins, and there was nothing in his expression that even remotely resembled ordinary human joy as he offered a steroidal thigh to the camera and flexed. He looked like he was trying to shit out a cactus.

"Is that what you want to look like? Really? That ain't riiight!" he cried.

Todd was always minting little neologisms that quickly made their way around school, becoming the currency of cool. "That ain't *riiight!*" my peers barked in stereo from the surrounding lockers. They were suddenly in a fierce competition to see who could laugh the loudest. I chuckled nervously. Todd had a way of joking where you weren't sure if you were in on the joke, or the joke itself. And if you weren't sure, that pretty much answered your question.

He strode down the hall, striking bodybuilding poses and shouting, "That ain't riiight!" As I saw the reverence accorded to him by the shrieking, flexing nerds he left in his wake, a new goal appeared on my horizon: I would become a jock, like Todd. If there was one place at our college prep school where you were finally let in on the joke, instead of being the joke, it was the locker room.

As I couldn't imagine accomplishing this objective on my own, I decided to once again entreat the Creator through one of his handlers—this time, Saint Thérèse, the "Little Flower." Her name was attached to a novena, a nine-day series of prayers, which allegedly provided a strong spiritual return on one's investment of time and credulity. My relationship with God at this point was like that of a scheming grandson to his billionaire grandfather. I had to somehow ease him out of a relatively negligible portion of his infinite bounty by dropping little hints about what I wanted, all while flying under his radar just enough so that he would never catch on to the mercenary nature of my supplications.

"He's a quiet one, doesn't ask for much," God would tell his right hand man, Saint Michael, as he noticed me on my knees in my bedroom through a hole in the heavenly nimbus. "Increase his vertical jump by seven inches, then let's get back to work on this African poverty thing."

Everyone made the team at my school, and so I sat at the lonely end of the bench, forgotten by all, except Todd Hunter. During time-outs he would walk all the way down to the end of the bench, gob in a Styrofoam cup, and hand it to me. Desperate to get off the bench, I shot hoops after hours every night until Andy, our wee, cross-eyed janitor, hit the lights, and then I shot in the dark, which actually made no difference in terms of my accuracy. When I tried to dribble, my hand and the ball behaved like the positive poles of two magnets. Plus, the rules confused me—I couldn't stop fouling my teammates during scrimmages, and when Coach K. called a play I usually wound up running around in circles until the ball hit me in the back of the head.

I tried to apply the same lessons my father had taught me about shooting a gun to shooting a basketball. I needed to pay less attention to how I was doing and more attention to the game itself. Then my performance would take care of itself. But I couldn't relax. I couldn't let go. I was unable to give my "clean best," as I called it—to lose myself in the game.

"You think too much," my father said. "That's the problem. The second you catch the ball, you gotta go to that other room in your head, the one with the sign outside the door that says No Thinking. Your subconscious."

This was a little too esoteric for me, and so I decided to give my mother's religion one last shot. To hell with the handlers: this time I went to God himself. I created what I called the "Sacrifice Tabulator." (No lie.) At the top of a piece of notebook paper I drew a basketball that emanated crude rays of light signifying its worthiness as a spiritual objective. At the bottom of the page I drew the first rung on a ladder. Then I began to perform good deeds. For each of these good deeds I drew another rung on the ladder, which, straight and sturdy, would eventually arrive at the basketball. At that point, the great hand of God was supposed to reach down and nudge all my airballs into the hoop. (In all fairness, God and I never actually shook hands on the deal.)

As I recall, the ladder wound up reaching the basketball pretty quickly, as I hadn't set the bar for a good deed very high. Called my brother a little asshole instead of a *Goddamn* little asshole? That counted for one rung. Washed my own filthy gym socks instead of passing them off to Mom? Two socks, two rungs! Unfortunately, the Supreme Being behaved pretty much like all the other beings I knew with power and good fortune. He held on to it, and I rode the pine all season.

To make matters worse, I was on the JV squad, which had to scrimmage against the varsity girls' team. I had to guard the shapely shooting guard with the high forehead and bouncing chest that I was achingly in love with. This was not what I had in mind when I fantasized about her sweaty body rubbing up against mine. *This will not do!* I cried inside as she sunk a three-point bomb in my face, chest-bumping her teammates and pointing at me as if to say, "Your ass is mine, Spaz!"

The fear of failure was in the air in our house. My father had inherited a small machine shop from his father, a bony preacher's son of German stock. For a few years there, we were like a family of tree-swinging monkeys, going from financial vine to financial vine. Sometimes, when we let go of the vine behind us, there was no vine swinging back at us from the other way. And so we were suspended, hanging, waiting.

My father saw the writing on the wall: if he didn't evolve the business fast we would plunge into poverty. He made the bold choice, against his father's wishes, to transform the machine shop into a rifle-barrel business. By my sophomore year, orders were picking up. H. Barrels was taking off. I watched in awe as success transformed him. He became both lighter and more substantial. He smiled a lot, when nothing funny had been said. Boxes of doughnuts appeared on the kitchen counter. My mother put the phone back on the hook.

What was his secret? Not prayer. I saw that now. Prayer was a consolation prize for those who didn't—who couldn't—make it.

Blessed are the meek, for theirs shall be the kingdom of God.

Prayer was for losers.

Late one night my junior year, I left my bed and drove an hour to the neighborhood where we'd lived before my parents uprooted us for a farmhouse in the country. I parked in the cul-de-sac where I'd once delivered the *Milwaukee Sentinel* every morning, and stole through the dawn-lit woods until I came upon a vast, gaping, nature-overridden hole in the earth. Once a gravel quarry, it served as a forbidden playground in my youth. I stood on the highest, most vertiginous cliff, where a wild childhood friend had once almost pushed me over the edge, grabbing the back of my T-shirt just as I began to fall.

I looked down.

If you look into your life at the right moment, with the right eyes, you will see right down into the middle of it. And you will know instantly and perhaps forever what the central and defining conflict and question of your life is. Usually that question or conflict can be summed up in one word: love, anger, family, grief, redemption. Standing there, at the peak of my youth, I knew what my word was: *success.* I saw into the depths of my own overriding ambition to make something out of myself, to make my life something other than what it was.

Something about the cool pre-sunlit air, and the open space before me, coaxed me fully out of myself, into the dawning light. In that moment I could scarcely admit to the passage of an hour, even during sleep, where my actions were not guided by the lure of, nor my mind not set upon the thought of, success, broadly defined here as the quest for better circumstances. I wanted to beat reality into shape. I wanted it to resemble my motives. I wanted it to obey me. I had no respect for it. I wanted to be its master. Ultimately, success meant being more in control of my life than my life was in control of me. In this, I thought I was like most people, that everyone's all-defining word meant to them what my word meant to me: the ability to make one's life do as it is told.

Later that winter, as we drove home from basketball practice, my father slid a cassette into the van's tape deck, thus initiating my conversion from Mom's Catholicism to his all-American belief system. He was amassing a small but growing library of self-help audiocassettes from various success artisans with comb-overs and mammon mystics who had shaken the unseen hand. He drove me to and from Hillcrest Academy every day, and like a rabbi and son unlocking the mysteries of the Torah we sat in silence while titles like *Acing Your Inner Demons* and *Triumph: A Road Map!* washed over us.

Dad and I gravitated toward the self-help sages who preached the gospel of subliminal reprogramming. A vast, unknowable substratum or wellspring of psychic energy, which could be tapped and brought into your service, the subliminal mind was akin to all of God's power and resources with none of his pesky divine will clinging to it. Instead of the well-guarded fortune of a supernatural Scrooge McDuck, the secret to becoming a winner was more like a cache of diamonds hidden in your own backyard. You just had to figure out where it was buried—the satchel of success was sunk deep within your own mind.

Soon a parcel arrived at our doorstep from Nighthawk, "the Cadillac of the self-help industry," as Dad called the company. Inside was a golden folio lined with a dozen black cassette tapes featuring subliminally layered inspirational messages. Side A: a numbingly banal soundtrack of ocean waves. Side B: throat-slittingly breezy light jazz. Each tape was labeled according to the individual loser's needs: *Make Money; Courage; More Joy.* I borrowed the tape entitled *Confidence!* and kept it on an endless loop.

The bleating seagulls, the crashing waves! The tinkling synth strings, the poor man's Kenny G horn! *The horror . . . the horror!*

Impatient with the tape's results, and appalled by its aesthetics, I decided to create my own subliminal messaging tape, one tailored to my specific needs. With the Beatles *Magical Mystery Tour* blasting from my boombox in the background, I pushed record on an old Casio tape deck and whispered inspirational nuggets like "You will score points! Believe in yourself!" However, I could never quite get the nuts and bolts of the operation down. Overeager, I would whisper too loud, and when I played the tape back, "Nothing can stop you! Go man go, drive to the hoop! Soar, boy, soar!" competed for my attention with "I am the walrus / Goo goo g' joob!"

Finally I got into a game and scored two points, and it went like this—and I know it went like this because to this day my father still reminds me of it. Without thinking (this is key) I stole the ball, pounded the length of the opposing team's floor, "And finally laid that miserable son-of-a-bitching thing in! You went into that other room in your head," my father thundered. "You didn't have time to think about it!"

I remember how the snowflakes whizzing across our van's windshield looked like stars slashing past the *Millennium Falcon* as it blasts into light speed. As we bounced over the train tracks he turned to me and said, "Try to miss. When you get the ball, tell yourself, 'There ain't no *way* I'm gonna make this shot.'"

Years earlier, my father had competed in the one-thousand-yard State Rifle match at Camp Perry. He whiffed enough of his initial shots to feel confident that he'd blown the entire match. With the pressure off, he noticed that he was carrying a little extra tension in his belly. He breathed it out. He felt a slight breeze on his face and adjusted his aim accordingly. He sensed the constriction in his shoulders—tautness, nervous energy. He relaxed a little. Let it go, whatever it was—probably the desire to win. Having gone through the necessary rituals somewhat by accident, he found himself in the zone without really knowing it. He began to plug away at the target, having a high old time.

"I almost shit my drawers when they told me I won the match," he said. "Try to miss! You know what I call this? The Power of Negative Thinking. When you can't do a goddamn thing right, just do the opposite of what you think you should do."

So I did. "Haubner, you're gonna brick this shot just like you always do, and everyone's gonna know it was nerves!" I'd tell myself at the free-throw line. Then I'd airball the shot. Instead of failing at succeeding, my usual MO, I began, thanks to the Power of Negative Thinking, to succeed at failing. Either way, that ball was not going in the hoop.

"Don't you love the game?" my father asked one evening, "For its own sake, not just because of how you feel when you play well?" My silence told him everything he needed to know. He turned off the van's tape deck, leaving our subliminal minds to their own devices. "You want to know what's the most important thing you can do in this life?" He was wearing an old denim coat, and there was black grease under his fingernails. There were tears in his eyes. "Find the one thing you love to do, and then do it, and keep doing it, and don't let anyone stop you, no matter what, not even me."

I knew then what my father's "one word" was, and that his word did not mean the same thing to him as mine meant to me. It did not mean controlling the outcome, but giving yourself over to the process. To do this you had to love something so much that you were willing to risk everything else for it. You had to care deeply about something other than yourself.

My father was a religious man after all. We did not have to live like a family of monkeys swinging from paycheck to paycheck. He could have gotten a decent-paying job at any machine shop in town. But he didn't want a decent-paying job. He wanted to do something that he loved. That's what gave him the courage to let go of his fears, to remain suspended in the unknown with the terrible truth that he could plunge at any moment and take us down with him. He had faith that the world would come to him, meet his reach from the other way—faith not in God, and not even in the subconscious. He had faith in himself. And what gave him this faith, genuinely rare among men, was a love so strong that it drew this natural introvert out of himself and into the world, where he eventually flourished as one of the world's foremost custom cut-rifled barrel makers.

My father had answered the question, How do you let go? with: For something other than yourself. When I realized this, I knew that there was nothing and no one that I truly loved. I lived my life based on fear and desire, in that order. I had no genuine passion for anything or anyone. It's hard to think of a moment in my life when I have felt more alone or worthless. Not only was I a failure, I was deeply selfish to boot.

A week later I had to guard Todd Hunter during practice. He caught the ball in the lane, pivoted, and blasted to the hoop. I tried to scramble out of his way and wound up fouling him. He pushed past me and took his place inside the lane for the next play. He snagged the pass again and tried the exact same move. He was challenging me. The second biggest player on the team had defied a similar challenge from Todd a week before. The episode ended with the two of them trading blows, and Coach K. made them spend the next day at school handcuffed together.

I fouled him again. He was quite an animal. Big, graceful, deadly. He moved less by will than as though some natural force were moving through him. He caught the ball a third time, squared up, and tried to power his way to the hoop. I gave him plenty of space, fully content to let him score, but I couldn't backpedal fast enough. He plowed into me and I bodychecked him. He did not lose the ball this time when he lost his balance. He hung on to it with one hand, holding it outward, his shoulders shaking with laughter.

Then he hurled it against the wall. The rubber-brick blast reverberated throughout the entire gym, which grew very quiet—all the way down to the other end, where the girls were scrimmaging.

Coach K. blew his whistle: "That's it for today!"

In the locker room, I scrambled to strip off my uniform and throw on my school clothes. I would skip showering that evening. As I dug my penny loafers from the bottom of my locker, I felt his presence behind me, along with a general dimming of my teammates' chatter. I was squatting before my locker, clutching my shoes. I couldn't stand up, because I knew that it would then begin. I did not want to do anything that might get me shackled to Todd Hunter for a day.

"Hey, Jack," he said. "You were all over me out there. Jumping up and down, waving your arms. You were like a little dirt monkey!"

He started banging on a row of lockers, screeching like an orangutan, imitating my defensive moves on the court. High-octane humor bullying.

"Dirt monkey!" someone shouted.

I knew the nickname would stick. I put on a big shit-eating grin and laughed with my teammates, and then, to avoid violence, I solidified my status as the team joke and barked like a monkey.

I sat at my bedroom desk for a very long time that evening, staring at a hunting knife my father had given me. We'd used it to skin a buck the previous fall. There was still a crusty speck of fur on the serrated saw edge opposite the ten-inch blade. I wrote a few kind words to myself in my journal, as though getting them out of my head and onto the page might advance the illusion that they had issued from an objective source.

Then I returned my full attention to the knife. I had thought that I'd outgrown my childhood fascination with weapons, but a recent crushing weariness had helped me to see the many guns and blades in our house in a new light. I waited for the right moment— then I sliced two deep wounds into the palms of both hands. This was to remind me—every single time I caught the basketball and felt a sting—that I could not fail anymore. It was now a matter of life and death.

The blood was out of control: I considered it the least I could do. I needed a wake-up call. I heard my father pacing around the hallway outside my room. H. Barrels had been featured in *American Rifleman* magazine, and he was impatient to share his copy with me.

He banged on my door, calling my nickname. "Magoo?"

"Just a minute," I said.

I waited for his footsteps to disappear down the hallway, and then I ducked into the bathroom. I washed the blood away, but it kept coming. I washed and washed, then I bandaged my palms, slipped back into my room, dropped my shirt to the floor, and engaged in that most perilous of teenage temptations: I stared at myself in the mirror. I catalogued my body's every flaw, but the main problem was that there just wasn't enough of it. I studied my hideous, ridiculous person: the man I'd been waiting for had never arrived. This was it. This was what I was stuck with. This was me. There was nothing more on the way.

Oversensitive, miniature, hopelessly average: this just wasn't how I was supposed to be. I was trapped in the hell realm of self-hate otherwise known as adolescence, and the only way out was not to grow big, but to grow *up*.

"I hate you," I said to the mirror. "I hate you, I hate you, I hate you."

My dad was standing in the doorway with his magazine. He walked over and put his hand on my shoulder.

I said, "I love you, Dad."

It surprised me. I hadn't planned this, and I'd never said it before. I had no idea where it came from, and I wasn't at all sure if I even meant it. It made me feel incredibly uncomfortable to mouth those words, yet I knew I had to. If I didn't love something, or someone, soon, something vital in me would be lost forever. I could already feel it, whatever it was, slipping away. My hatred was getting ahead of me, laying tracks in the wrong direction, hurtling me toward a future defined entirely by the past.

"I know, Magoo," he said. We stared at each other, and ourselves, in the mirror. If I was clueless about whether or not I loved him—or anything at all—he knew better. My father had faith in me.

By midseason my senior year, I was just beginning to enjoy being in my body, like a silent-film comic who turns his awkwardness into an asset. If I hadn't grown much, I'd started to grow into what little I had. I developed a goofy, eccentric persona, a spaz still, but a spaz who, upon doing something idiotic, was now beating everybody to the punch line. I wasn't a joke: I was *funny*. But as I would discover, a fool and his funny are soon parted.

Late in the fourth quarter of a tie game, a loose ball bounced into my path. I dove for it, skidded on my knees, shot to my feet—still dribbling—did a 180 spin move around a big all-conference power forward and shot down court. There was nothing but clean hardwood ahead.

All-conference did not pursue me. No one did. I must have been moving very quickly. Suddenly I was alone with my destiny. I remember the crowd roaring, carrying me, like a tidal wave hoisting a surfer onto its shoulders. Something was not quite right, it was all too easy, but the momentum was great, and there was no stopping me.

This was my moment.

I scored a left-handed finger-roll layup. Before my Reeboks even hit the ground, I was spinning around and raising my hand for incoming high fives. Todd was right there, his face crumpled in agony. My teammates were closing in, screaming at me. The cheerleaders for the other team were joyously airborne.

I looked up. The scoreboard clicked over—we were now down by two points.

I'd scored on the wrong basket.

Spaz rides again!

When I was a kid, I took play quite seriously. I would choose one subject of inquiry or interest—or rather, it seemed to choose me—and then exclusively devote myself to it for an undisturbed length of time. First I was into dinosaurs, and then reptiles. I read everything I could about stegosauruses, pterodactyls, and T. rexes, and then I captured grass snakes in the backyard and nurtured little green lizards in an aquarium. When *Raiders of the Lost Ark* came out I transformed into a mini Indiana Jones forever in search of the perfect rope that would crack like a whip. Then I became obsessed with World War II and spent hours picking off imaginary Nazis with sticks that vaguely resembled an M1 carbine.

I still remember that feeling of *becoming* the things I loved to do. I also remember the shift, the night I began to slip away from myself. It happened in eighth grade, as I studied a yearbook photo of my older sister's high school class. *I want to be like Tommy York*, I thought. *He's really popular and he's great at sports.* I began to worry a whole lot about what people thought of me. I wasn't sure what I liked anymore. It depended on what the kids around me were into. I applied the same depth of passion I had once reserved for my own interests to getting good at the things that would make others take an interest in me.

I forgot how to play.

Instead of taking seriously the things that I loved to do, I took myself seriously. I wanted to be somebody. First an athlete, then a philosopher and a writer, then a comedian and a film director. As the years passed, I gave my life to each of these pursuits, waiting to become successful by somehow willing myself to be gifted at things that I wasn't even very good at. My sole passion was for success itself, which I felt would define me.

It has been my strange and ironic karma that through my efforts to make something out of myself, I have somehow failed my way into a spiritual practice whose defining teaching is that all things are empty of a "self" that we can make into anything at all. From the Buddhist point of view, the quest for success was never my defining motive. I was driven by something less personal, more fundamental: fear of the emptiness I felt within, and the desire to fill that emptiness with something, anything.

Most of us feel this hole within, a profound lack, and our deepest impulses in life are often just attempts to fill it. We want to become whole. Yet there is always an emptiness, a natural void, at our core that never lets us finish the task of creating a substantial, enduring identity, something that we can definitively call *me*. We yearn to exist with absolute autonomy, but because of this gap within we are compelled by human nature to keep moving, experiencing, growing. We are incapable of either becoming something solid on the inside, or creating something permanent on the outside, in order to find completion.

Sooner or later, what we all learn is that the void within us can never be completely filled, because it's not ours to fill. It belongs to everybody and nobody at the same time. It's that which we all share, but no one owns, like the abandoned rock quarry I used to love standing in front of, feeling as vast and open as the space before me. Ultimately you can't fill it, control it, develop it, or live without it. It's who you are when you forget yourself completely, and where you go when you're lost in the act of doing something you love. Through it, dreams enter you at night and answers come to you when you're not thinking. It's where *I* and *you* stop, and *we* begins.

The greatest mistake I have made in my life is conflating success with fulfillment. They are not mutually exclusive, but one is never a reliable indicator of the other. Where success often comes down to gaming this or that system in order to solidify and expand your sense of self, fulfillment means living vitally and being open to failure, because you can't dictate the outcome of a challenge that requires you to truly open yourself up to risk. And here's the rub: there is no fulfillment without risk. You can find success in life by controlling the variables, and all of society will pat you on the back and hand you cigars, but unless you have been brought to the brink of yourself, to the edge of the void—unless you have followed the pull in your gut instead of the smell of money or the sound of the crowd and all those glittering vistas—you will always feel the call of the void, the need to love something greater than yourself and to risk everything for it, and you will hate yourself for not following this inner call and letting it guide you forward, unsure though your steps may be.

After my botched basket, Todd was right there in my face, towering and implacable. He belittled me with his confident gaze, and then proceeded to win the game. He stormed the lane, drew the foul, hit a free throw, purposely bricked the next one, soared for the rebound, and nailed the put-back at the buzzer.

After the game, Coach K. swept into the locker room. "This is what basketball is all about. I love that kind of effort. You give it your all, and the rest is up to the gods." He was referring to me, not Todd, and he patted my shoulder to make his point. Then he left, the team parted, and I heard Todd's footsteps collapsing the distance between us. I turned to face him—the embodiment of all I thought I needed in life, everything I was certain I lacked.

I wish that back then I had been able to tell Todd, my teammates, and myself what it truly means to be a man, a human being, how hard it is, how rewarding, how different than the collective fantasy of "more" that we were being fed, and feeding each other, at Hillcrest High. I wish I could stand before them now, all forty years of me, and share what I've learned the hard way: *the worship of success thwarts true fulfillment.*

But I knew none of this then. I barely knew myself, and what I did know, I did not like. And so when Todd got in my face, I gave him what he wanted, which was not what any of us needed, least of all me. Because he was successful, and success was the standard by which I judged myself, I played jester to his court king and made like the spastic dirt monkey I was. I hopped up and down, drummed the lockers with my fists, and let out a primal scream that welled up from the void within.

3

The Divine Truth of a Kiss

To be read with several glasses of white wine and Billie Holiday's "I'll Be Seeing You" playing in the background

I just turned forty. My pubes are going gray, and when I stand in front of the mirror I see someone who kind of looks like me, but has been left in the sun and rain a little too long. But it's not just my body that's changing. Something has begun to grow large and heavy inside of me (other than my prostate). It's my past, which exerts a greater pull on my thinking the older I get. I've begun to experience regret, which is the mistake of applying the wisdom that comes with age to the past instead of the present.

Good news! Sort of. Recently I discovered a cure for middle-aged melancholy, a reminder that youth only looks good from the healthy distance afforded by age. I was cleaning out a closet when I found a sheaf of papers an ex-girlfriend printed out for me when we broke up—every e-mail I ever sent her, over three hundred pages of sappy, maudlin, desperate, bizarre, passive-aggressive, and, perhaps worst of all, poorly written drivel.

I was broken when I wrote these e-mails. But so what? We're all broken. This is the First Noble Truth in Buddhism: everyone's broken. If you take these two words seriously, as I did not at the time, then you know that our brokenness doesn't need fixing. It needs company. I used to think that being an adult meant being self-sufficient. These days I think it means realizing that the self is never sufficient. That's just not the way we're built.

I wrote these e-mails in my midtwenties. I'd grown out of my Catholic schoolboy phase only a few years earlier, ravenous for physical love. Yet each sexual conquest only led to more desire, which now had no framework to contain it, for when I lost my virginity I also lost the religion that had kept my desire in check. And so I made a religion out of love itself, with the hope that the right girlfriend would guide me to an understanding of my body and desires through hers.

That's a lot to put on a woman.

This project reached its inevitable conclusion when I met June, an older actress who had just broken up with her boyfriend of ten years. His haunting presence was most pronounced in the bedroom, where I learned that he was epically endowed. ("It was almost too much," she told me, holding her hands about a foot apart. It was that "almost" that got me.) He knew how to physically connect with June in ways that helped her escape her tortured self-consciousness—a fact she didn't fully appreciate until she met me, his opposite. The thing that I was looking for in her, she had already found and lost in someone else. I was a constant reminder of what she also needed, and so couldn't provide.

As girl-boy setups go, it was almost perfectly bad.

But in the beginning it was so, so good. She was fresh to LA from South Carolina, one of those tormented transplants who leaves behind a story that is far more interesting than any she could tell onscreen. She wore bright linen sundresses, taught a free yoga class in the park, and sang songs in bed that she wrote for me. I always felt like I was getting a tan just by being in the same room as her.

"I'm all woman, baby!" she would cry, and indeed, it seemed to me that she'd invented her own gender, as though before her there had only been something vaguely womanlike.

With her previous boyfriend—he of the big strong hands, a computer-tech roadie for Pearl Jam—she was relaxed and inspired. I brought out something unhinged in her. She could never be herself around me. I was needy, and too proud to admit it. I homed in on her weaknesses, her resistance to abstract thought and the fact that she was not well read. She attacked me for being trapped in my head. I begged her to show me the way out. Over a series of unforgettable dates—including the night we spent high and lost (one followed the other) in the Santa Monica Mountains—she requested a simple, sincere manifestation of my love as the answer to what we were both seeking.

"No woman has the key to her own heart," she said. "Why else would we put up with men?" I searched inside myself for that key with all the patience of a cop pawing a suspect for contraband. "It's not about you, baby," she tried to explain.

When we broke up a year later, she capped off a series of recent kindnesses with one final selfless gesture of the sort that she had been seeking from me all along. She handed me a folder with all the e-mails we'd ever exchanged and said that she loved the way I wrote. She always had sharp instincts, and her instinct here was that the things I couldn't express to her through actions had been there on the page the whole time. And so they must have existed somewhere inside me.

"You're a nonfiction writer," she said.

I've been rereading these e-mails, and I'm starting to think that the secret to a happy middle age lies not in finally seeing what you've been doing wrong all these years, but in discovering that you've been blind to what's really been happening all along. I finally see our relationship through her eyes: the words she learned for my benefit, her sincere stabs at a love poem. At the time I thought she was blowing me off with her one-sentence replies asking me to explain something. Now I realize that she was giving me space to be myself, to blossom on the page, where I felt most at home. I was always trying to become the perfect partner for her, or turn her into the perfect partner for me, but was there ever anything other than this fantasy of perfection that stood between us in the first place? Every relationship has a life of its own. If you chase after your ideal of what it should be, you miss out entirely on what it is.

Fortunately, our love occasionally caught me by surprise. In one of her longest e-mails she recounted our first kiss. I'd spent the whole awkward evening at her house trying to impress her, which is the lover's version of quicksand: the harder you struggle the deeper you sink. We fall in love when we catch people in the act of fully being themselves, and never when they are trying to convince us of who they are.

"Really? You like Ella Fitzgerald too?" she said. "What's your favorite song?"

"Strange Fruit?"

"Yeah, that's Billie Holiday."

She baked me salmon with capers in a cream sauce and we ate at a small table in her kitchen. She set a place for her cat, who jumped up on the table and tongued his food beside me. The whole house smelled like marijuana. June didn't seem ripped, though she'd been hitting the bong all evening. She just seemed more and more like herself. That's what I loved about her—that naturalness, even (or especially) in the presence of vice.

"Oh, well, we have to try this!" She uncorked the bottle of cheap wine I'd brought and became a perfect bonfire of multiple intoxications. Yet she never lost her Southern charm.

"A guy asked me to pee on him once. On like the second date!" she said.

"Did you do it?"

"Are you kidding me? Of course."

"I'm not sure if you're joking."

"I want to show you something."

We went out on her porch. She lived in the mountains in To-panga Canyon. Insects clicked in the moonlight, the scent of orange blossoms floated on a cool breeze.

"Can you feel that?" she said. "Doesn't it feel great?"

"Doesn't what feel great?"

"This," she said, gesturing.

She had been talking all evening. She was an actress, and it was tiring playing the role of her best self. Now she needed a partner to complete the scene.

"Didn't you want to show me something?" I asked.

She sighed. "I already did."

We went back inside.

I took my keys and wallet off the kitchen counter. She wanted to look at a Thomas Guide with me because she didn't know where Studio City was and she had an audition in the morning, so I sat down with her on the couch and showed her how to get to the 101 Freeway. At one point I opened my mouth to yawn, and when I closed it my lips were on hers. I'm still not sure how this happened, how much time it took, who made the first move. I do know this: you never know what the next moment is going to bring you.

Never.

Some people just know how to kiss. They take you up against their mouth and hold you there, wordlessly speaking of and breathing into you everything that is inside of them. When our lips touched, my consciousness became as soft as our kiss, and I *knew* her, as they say in the Bible when speaking of sex. My body couldn't truly know itself until it was up against hers, and vice versa. In knowing each other we knew ourselves.

A mouth is empty, it's an opening, and the divine truth of a kiss is this: when two openings truly meet, somehow they complete each other, and where there was nothing but lack, now there is a whole. And yet, it was June who also taught me that love does not make us perfect. It is the gift by which we share our brokenness with each other.

I chased after the spontaneous bliss of that first kiss the whole year we were together. Eventually I tried to recreate the connection chemically. One evening, at a twenty-four-hour dance party in the desert, as the ecstasy we'd taken kicked in along with the DJ's ribcage-rattling set, June zipped us up in our tent, put her feet in my lap, and I looked in her eyes and saw a pair of jewels that have been heated and are changing colors. Everything was illuminating as myself, as my Zen teacher, the Roshi, would later say. A shiver flashed up my spine like a lit fuse, I went bliss-mute, and June, never one to pass up a captive audience, took off her shirt, touched her chest, and gave me her philosophy on life and love, reworked here with a little of the poetic license that she always afforded me:

Everyone is born with a heart torn wide open and a little trickle of love dribbling out. The point is not to fix ourselves so that we're perfect for others, or to fix others until they're perfect for us. The point is to press our wounds together, to fill each other with all the pain and tears and weirdness that flows out, all those dark and vibrant energies that long to be free, and to merge with the same in others.

We sat across from each other for six hours, holding hands and rolling on ecstasy, a drug used by psychotherapists in the seventies as a tool to help married couples open up. Boundaries fell away. Everything was resolved between us while we were high. And then we sobered up and everything fell apart.

The following morning, as familiar arguments began to cloud the artificial light briefly cast on our relationship by the ecstasy, I began to shed my clothes. While driving. At eighty-plus miles an hour. Not to be outdone, she pulled her sundress over her head and kicked off her sandals and soon we were naked together. We were big on forced spontaneity, but really, I think being naked in front of each other was what we were aiming for all along, though to truly do so would have required far more than just removing our clothes.

"I don't need a circus act, I need a partner," she said. It was the first time I'd seen her break down into tears outside of acting class.

We each took a Prozac to smooth our descent from the drug high, and rode together in silence, naked, like a parody of her desire to navigate a course through life with someone she loved. She had a saying that became a kind of mantra toward the end, a way of whiting out my blacker and blacker moods. She said it for the first time with tears streaming down her face as we drove a straight line through the searing Nevada desert.

"Trust and love, Jack. Trust and love."

Not long after, I got the call. "I want to give you something," she said.

We met at the Bourgeois Pig, the same Los Feliz coffee shop I'm sitting in right now as I read these e-mails through wet eyes that I'm trying to hide from all these assholes with creative facial hair and thrift-store belt buckles. People talk about love at first sight. They don't talk about the death of love at first sight, but that's surely what I saw when she walked through the door and the smile left her face. We took a booth in back and shared a pot of Moroccan mint tea. She handed me the folder of e-mails, which surprised me, and then dumped my ass, which did not.

Here, among all these hipsters? I thought.

I call this the Moment of Death: the instant you know it's truly over. We'd dumped each other before—it was even a kind of ritual—but this time I knew it would stick. She was a very private person. The fact that she'd ended our relationship in front of a barista with a Rollie Fingers mustache told me that she now considered me part of the crowd, just another face. She needed the safety of strangers to make me one of them again.

Only once during our brief exchange did she cross the formidable gulf between us, to say: "I never needed you to prove yourself when we were together. I needed you to forget yourself."

"I don't think you know what you need, that's the problem."

"Commitment. That's what I need. But all you've got are gestures."

She left me with a pot of tea too big for one man to finish alone, and after a few moments of shock I suddenly realized that there was no one sitting across from me to project my fears and fantasies onto. No one to love or hate. I never needed her more than the moment that I realized she was gone forever. What made it so painful was that I'd wasted the whole relationship trying to win her over, so we'd never really gotten to know each other. I was heartbroken by a mystery.

There was a hole where she had torn herself off of me, and the cold world was howling through. The wound was open. That is the only time you can change, and it is the hardest time to change. You cannot bear to look in that hole, to look inside yourself. Miss this chance, however, and you will wander the world haunted by your demons, which have been sealed inside you, behind the once open wound. Until you meet someone special. Someone you could love. And she opens you up again. And out come those same demons.

Karl Marx famously said that religion is the opiate of the masses. Fine by me. You have to find a way of working with your open wounds, and spiritual practice worked for me. It served as a kind of numbing agent that allowed me to go deeper into my suffering without intensifying it. I was beginning to see that my potential was nearing its expiration date and on its way to becoming an unfulfilled dream. I needed a way to make peace with my mediocrity, mistakes, and male-pattern baldness. But most importantly I needed a way of looking at the world that was as big as the biggest love I'd ever lost. I needed to know that the connection I'd felt with June was not limited to her alone, and that in losing her I did not lose everything, which was how it felt at the time.

You are not alone. This is what meditation taught me. It stilled all the voices in my head so that I could connect with the world around me, just as I connected to June with that first kiss. Coincidentally, she was the one who first taught me to how to meditate.

After our naked desert drive, she gave up trying to talk to me. Instead, she would sing. A western sycamore with a shimmering two-hundred-foot canopy towered in the canyon behind her house. Its trunk was a personable giant covered with burl-and-bark faces; its great roots puffed and settled above the ground like octopus tentacles. When the city voted to cut it down, dozens of locals rallied around the tree and tied ribbons and notes of appreciation to its swaying boughs, which touched the earth, reached for the sky, and stretched out in a fanning circle like Leonardo da Vinci's Vitruvian Man.

You could say that this tree aged well. It did what you're supposed to do as you accumulate layers of life: gnarled, unique, it had grown around, in upon, and through its flaws to become something both crooked and true. Just being around this great being made you wiser. June found Buddhism before I did. A few days before we broke up she led me to the Prayer Tree, as we called it, and gave me my first meditation lesson. It was morning, and she scaled the branches in her silk pajamas with a song she'd scribbled on a notepad. I nestled into the tree's serpentine roots, crossed my legs, and unintentionally mirrored Shakyamuni Buddha when he found true peace under the Bodhi tree.

She ordered me to listen: "Do not pay any attention to the words. Just sit inside the music."

Ostensibly about the tree, her song asked the listener to never attach to the things he loves, which sooner or later must leave him. She was teaching me how to be without her. The end was coming and she wanted to prepare me for it. If ever there was anyone who could help me get over her, it was her.

"If one-half of meditation is being open to things, the other half is learning to let go," she explained.

We'd gotten into a fight around sunrise, and then made love, and then fought while making love—such was our love-hate relationship that we often loved and hated each other in the same moment. I tried to follow my breath and be in my body, as she'd taught me, but I was throbbing with unresolved emotion. (Is there any other kind?) I couldn't be still. My limbs ached for lack of movement, unlike the limbs of the tree, which hung silently all around me, thrumming with life.

I thought, *If you can't be alone with yourself, you're going to make a really shitty partner for someone else.*

I wanted to follow her up that tree. I wanted to fuck away all our problems. I wanted her to have my baby. I wanted to grab her and fling us both from the highest branch. I can still remember her voice. It was slightly imperfect, one note off, and that's what I loved about it. There was a gap between what she hoped to convey and her ability to pull it off, and she sang her heart out to make up the difference.

Is there something beneath all of our voices that is this pure, this consistent, this trustworthy? No wonder we fall in love over and over again. We're looking for this song in each other, and in ourselves. But we'll never find it if we're not ready to receive it. So we go to work on the meditation cushion, in our churches, with our therapists and priests and each other. We keep trying, no matter how hard it gets. Because everyone's heart is like a tiny broken radio. And every morning when we wake up we have to tinker with it all over again, just to get it right, so that those brief snatches of beautiful music can escape through all the static.

That morning, as she sang for me and the tree—both of us about to get the ax—a little bit of that music got through. I heard it not just in her voice, but in the breeze through the leaves, the chirping birds, the blood pumping in my ears as I sat still under the tree. For once I felt like I was living exactly at the speed of life, from moment to moment, letting the past go and the future be. I've felt it again over the years, but the moment I sit down alone to capture the meaning of this divine truth, I cannot find the words. I had hoped to find them today reading through these e-mails, but there are no words to describe the moment when words become unnecessary. This is a terrifying moment for a writer, for it is the moment when you become unnecessary, too. And yet it is also the moment that you touch the source of all inspiration.

That pretty much sums up how I felt during my year with June—unnecessary and inspired. But as she once said, "It's not about you, baby." She was right about that. Reading through these old e-mails makes me want to cut out my tongue so I never speak another word. Yet there's something sweet about both of our e-mails together. There are moments when we come together on the page and speak with one voice. There are no words to describe it, except, perhaps, the ones she used to sign off her final e-mails:

Trust and love.

4

Jumping the Wall

The evening began with a marijuana joint at sundown. I was alone at the monastery, sitting cross-legged on a woody bluff overlooking our sutra hall. The sky was the roiling hue of spilled orange juice, and the Santa Ana winds were blasting in from the east, bringing with them that prickly desert mentality of survival and desire.

A few weeks earlier, as I passed through the kitchen, the monastery cook looked up from the chopsticks he was inexplicably lighting on fire over a stove flame and barked, "Happy birthday, Jefe, want some pot?"

I was shocked, but not by the discovery that he smoked pot. In fact I would have been surprised if drugs were not a key ingredient in his brain chemistry. Tall and gangly, Ernie was always running his sentences together, and was given to arbitrary fits of conversation-halting laughter that sounded like the bark of a small dog underfoot. "Want some pot? SOME POT? Some Northern . . . Lights . . . POT? Come with me to my room . . . ha Ha HA—*Haahahahahahahaha*—HAAAAAAAA!"

Rather, I was shocked because he broke, and at the same time made me conscious of, an important unspoken understanding at our monastery: if you're going to do something against the rules, don't get caught, and for Christ's sake don't tell anyone about it, especially not the head monk. Because then he's got to do something about it. And it's just plain rude of you to put him in that position.

So I did something about it: I accepted his offer with a forced wink, making myself complicit in his misdeed so that I wouldn't have to confront him. Roshi had recently made me *shika*, or head monk. This meant that after three years of griping about the monastic leadership, I awoke one morning to find those same complaints being leveled at me. Unfortunately, being unqualified for the job is one of the chief qualifications for getting it: shika is a training position, which you must grow into. And so I had to literally evolve on the spot, in front of everyone. I had to make myself up as I went along, drawing upon resources I did not yet possess, my every mistake magnified.

After a week of this, I stole behind the showerhouse and held fire to a cigarette that I'd bummed from a nun. I hadn't smoked in five years. *I deserve this*, I thought. With that inhale, I realized something key about men with power: when you're called upon to give more than you have, you often feel justified in taking more than you should. Powerful men, like the rest of us, must hold themselves in balance. How will they offer more of themselves to the world if they don't take more of the world for themselves? To take more risks, they must take more liberties. Such, I realized, is the moral calculus of great men with great flaws.

Of course, drugs were strictly forbidden at the monastery—by me, I guess. But wasn't I, as the head monk, just a little bit above the rules? After all, they weren't etched in stone by the hand of some divine Phyllis Schlafly. They were *upayas* or "skillful means" meant to aid in a practice that leads to game-changing insights into the root of human suffering—and not, in exchange for good behavior, to some celestial tomorrow, with saints, cherubs, or eighty virgins waving signs for you like airport limo drivers at the afterlife arrival gate. It was this understanding of "rules as tools" that first drew me to Zen practice. As an ex-Catholic, I was done with traditional religious notions of good and evil. I was resentful for all those years I wasted fretting over how God felt about my erections.

Besides, I thought, it's often the violation of rules that triggers the greatest liberation. Transgression jolts the mind into a fresh awakening, freeing it from the fetter of conventional thinking. In the words of Bodhidharma, the sixth-century founder of Zen Buddhism: "When one transcends right and wrong, he is truly right." Bodhidharma also said, "I only talk about seeing your [true] nature. I don't talk about sex. . . ."

I took a power puff from the joint and forgot what I was thinking about, except that it had to do with sex. The first thing I want to do when I'm high is have sex with all the wrong people, which is to say anyone who will have sex with me when I'm high.

I smoked half my birthday joint and fell asleep under a pine tree, its boughs winding upward like a feathery green staircase; woke up, smoked the other half, lost consciousness once more. When I awoke again, Kuru, the monastery cat, was preparing to lick my face. His big pink tongue unscrolled and quivered wetly from a crooked column of friendly fangs. He was smiling like some kind of lunatic, his cloudy eyes resolving themselves like two mini Magic 8 Balls reaching a conclusion. His damp nose looked weirdly edible, like a berry from another solar system.

I rolled to one side, yanked up my sweatshirt, and let him lick my back with his coarse, perfect tongue. "Meow, meow, meow," I said to him.

"*There there*," he said back, in my mind. "*It's all good . . . it's all good, homeboy.*"

Crows were committing suicide all around me—or so it seemed. Wild winds were tearing free and holding aloft black shingles from the sutra-hall roof. They spent several moments suspended and flapping before kamikazeing through treetops and dying with a thud on the forest floor. Dizzy, I stood up. My innards and brain fell into alignment, and the universe reached out and shook my hand: *Hey there partner. You high!* My heart beat like a big kettledrum: *Bong! Bong! Bong!—You! The! Man!* I shook my fists and shouted—"RAHHHHH!"—and the wet-leafed echoless forest swallowed my rebel yell whole. Strolling down our gravel driveway made me feel even more on track.

But where was I going?

To the office, for the Honda keys.

The pit of my stomach was like a divining rod: taut, lucid, leading me forward a little too fast.

I was jumping the wall.

Jumping the wall is an ancient unspoken tradition in Zen. After *kaichin*, or closing gong, restless young monks the world over sneak out to low hanging branches and struggle their way up and over the monastery wall to the booze, breasts, and bongos beyond. In Zen, true liberation means that you attach to nothing, including the means of your emancipation—Zen practice itself. You must leap over or transcend the tradition, lest it become one more human institution imprisoning you with its protocol. Like each half of the yin-yang symbol, the Zen monastery contains within itself the seed for that which it is not. The custom of wall jumping is a trapdoor into the stormy, fleshy elements of the human world that the monochromatic monastic rituals and disciplines are defined against.

We all have our walls to jump. Whenever you rebel against the explicit intention you've set for your life, you jump the wall. You jump the wall of your career when you call in sick and sneak off to the outlet mall. You jump the wall of your marriage when you secretly binge on porn. Those potato chips? Jumping the wall of your commitment to health, you fatty.

Perhaps by injecting your routine existence with trace amounts of these tiny revolts you are inoculating yourself against greater future temptations. Then again, maybe you are lowering your immunity to trouble and exposing your better self to lethal infection. There's no saying how far you'll go once you've stepped outside the protective boundaries that define you, or if you'll ever be able to come back to yourself in quite the same way again.

I drove the Honda down the mountain switchbacks, the twinkling valley spread beneath me like a sequined dress fanned out on a dark motel-room floor. To my right, riding shotgun, was Ethel, my conscience. The pot had eased her out of my subconscious and into the passenger's seat. Her thick arms were crossed; her jaw, made out of a kind of pink steel, was solidly set, like Mike Mulligan, the steam-shovel operator. She was wearing neither a blouse nor a bra and, as I recall, where normally there would be breasts, she had a pair of bowling-ball-sized, hairy-knuckled fists. When I needed it the most, pot had turned my conscience into a caricature.

You're thinking with your dick! she cried.

I thought about this. *It's more like my dick is thinking for me, and doing a pretty spotty job of it.*

During a recent airport run I'd driven through the outskirts of town, where adult and Christian bookstores competed for the same down-and-out demographic. It was comforting seeing these age-old enemies in such close proximity, duking it out once again, like Wile E. Coyote and the Road Runner. Idling at a red light, I saw a neon sign in a strip mall: Massage. A legitimate bodywork establishment has a discernable storefront, is not open at 10:00 p.m., and does not feature iron bars over its darkened windows. Once you've patronized one of these jack shacks (as I had, a decade earlier—the only time I'd ever paid for anything even related to sex, thank you very much), you can always spot them.

I parked in front of the neon sign and gave myself one last chance to be my mother's good son. But I'd just spent three years of self-slaughter in the monastic foxhole. I longed to touch and be touched. Sometimes you just plain need human hands traveling across your skin, past your waistband. Sometimes you need your lever pulled.

I suggested to Ethel that after a certain age, if your sex life is defined largely by you touching yourself, it might actually be healthier if you just pay someone to do the job for you. Her fist-breasts quivered. She so wanted to punch me: *But what about her, whoever she is, on the other side of that door? Is buying her flesh good for her?*

I'm not paying her *for* her body, I'm paying her to *receive* my affection, I reasoned. I craved a romantic sexual encounter with someone with whom I was not romantically involved. I could go to a bar, seduce a woman (if I was lucky—which I never am, not with these big ears and small feet), leave her bed the following morning with an awkward goodbye, and be her emptiest sexual encounter of the year. Or, I could be a prostitute's most intimate and loving. I wanted to offer a little tenderness to another human being, and who better to receive it than a woman who probably very rarely experienced tenderness of any kind? You cannot buy intimacy, but if you're the one paying you can *give* it, right? I was a good guy doing a bad thing. What better visitor for a woman probably steeling herself at that very moment against the possibility that a bad guy was coming to do bad things to her?

My heart was pounding, my head was swimming, and yet I was still erect. There was red blood enough for every organ! I had one last chance to turn back before pushing through the big iron door—and so, dear reader, we've both reached the point of no return.

Stop here?

Come with me?

I entered what looked like a parody of a dentist's waiting room. There was a card table strewn with *Us Weekly* magazines; a plastic vase sprouting plastic tulips the searing yellow of a struck match. It was a ridiculous façade, the waiting room equivalent of

Groucho Marx glasses and a synthetic mustache. *See, officer? This is a legitimate massage establishment!*

At the head of the room, behind a sliding glass window, a rumpled-looking geezer fixed me with a gaze of intense concentration. I thought he was trying to shatter the glass between us telepathically. There was a blur of movement and the crack of a flyswatter—a slime-string of organic matter was now boogered across the windowpane. The pride on his face vanished as he looked from his kill to me.

"You been here before?" he said, squinting through granny glasses that were attached to a gold chain that looped around his neck and matched a second gold chain glinting from a tousle of chest hair.

"Nope. No sir. This is my first time. I'm a virgin!"

He studied me. Looking at him was like gazing at the picture of Dorian Gray and seeing me in fifty years. He was scowling, prudish, frail, hair tentacles clutching his oily gray skull. He had the pinched, devastated look of someone who works at a place that brokers in the very vice that ravaged him long ago, and in which he now rather haughtily refuses to indulge.

He was trying to figure out if I belonged there.

So was I.

Right before I moved to the monastery I visited a similar massage parlor in LA. I was stopped at a similar sliding window, in a similar waiting room, by an obese Chinese woman with moles running up her neck like pegs in a rock-climbing wall. She was so convinced that I didn't belong there that she convinced me too, and I left. (She kept jabbing her finger at me: "You cop? Cop, cop, cop?") I drove to the monastery with a clean conscience and never looked back.

Until today.

"Forty dollars. That's my price. That gets you through the door," the old man said. "Okay? Is that clear?"

"Yes."

"That's my price. Forty dollars. Whatever else goes on back there has nothing to do with me. Okay, guy?"

I held out my Visa card.

"We don't take *plastic*!" he said.

Inside my wallet were six crisp one-hundred-dollar bills—all of which belonged to my teacher. The following morning I planned on joining my monk peers in LA for a celebration, where I would hand our teacher, the Roshi, the cash on our behalf: part of a weird custom where we give him money from the monastery bank account—money that he has basically earned by leading our retreats—and pretend that it's a gift from us, only to have him nod solemnly in great thanks and then hand the money right back so that we can return it to the monastery bank account.

Fortunately I had a hundred dollars of my own (two months' worth of monk's allowance). I slid two twenties under the glass window. The old pimp ferried me down a low-ceilinged hallway, lined on either side by numbered doors. It was feral and dark, like a meaty tube. The floor felt uneven, the murky reddish atmosphere hot and thick, as though I was passing through the pulsing interior of some Hieronymus Boschian being, my butterfly-collared boatman and I just free-floating radicals in its mucousy bloodstream.

Hold it together! You're still high.

The old man deposited me behind the only open door. The smell of bleach was overwhelming, like a slaughterhouse at cleaning time. I stripped down to my boxers, sat on the massage table, and stared down the length of my body. There as usual were my monkey-thin thighs. I always try to introduce women to, say, my sense of humor before I show them my legs, but unless I cracked a joke right as she walked through the door, the first thing she'd see would be these hairy flagpoles, which could very well send her back out the door.

I took my wallet from my pants and hid it in my shoe. It felt like a bad omen if a prostitute made off with my teacher's gift money.

Already I mistrusted and was terrified of this creature I would soon be naked before—not an auspicious beginning to what was supposed to be our deep and meaningful *Lifetime Movie of the Week* sex romp. The room was nondescript, more like an idea of a room than the real thing. There was nothing to look at, nothing to pretend to think about, and I was getting nervous sitting there on that morgue-white bedsheet in my underwear, as though waiting for a doctor to bring back the results of a very serious test.

Is that skeezy geezer a cop? Is this all part of an undercover vice-squad sting? I could see the headline now: *Pervert Monk Jack Nabbed at Jack Shack!*

I had seen enough *60 Minutes*–type exposés to know what I was in for. One trim and trembling leg would broach the doorway, followed by the tiny torso and enormous blinking eyes of a Laotian Lolita, working off her illegal voyage to the States one porcine, hatchet-faced customonster at a time.

What have I become?

But it was too late to turn back now. Tonight I would see just how far I had come from my backward Catholic upbringing, where sex was treated like guns—"Dangerous! Steer clear!"—and guns were treated like sex: "Okay to experiment with, as long as you're safe." I lowered my eyes and held them to the door, like a bullfighter waiting for the gate to open, for his spectacular and devastating fate to buck through.

The doorknob clicked—there was a velvety swish as two bare feet glided across the carpet. I was staring at them sideways, a comma of drool trickling down my cheek. I had passed out cold.

I sat up, and if my eyes adjusted to the woman before me, my mind did not. *Holy matriarch!* I thought.

She was easily double my age. It was as though the missing Filipina cast member from the *Golden Girls* had hobbled through the door: "Surprise!" followed by a sinister laugh track as she pitches her dentures into a martini glass with a wink.

This woman had been around the block. In fact, she'd probably helped build the block, deadlifting bags of concrete with those short thick legs. She fussed around inside a little overnight pack festooned with cartoon circus-animal stickers. Out came her hand-sanitizer bottle, which she vigorously emptied into her palms, smacking them together and working up a lather while taking me in with a *Well, whadda we got today?* expression.

"Where are you from?" I asked. Just a couple of archetypes, the monk and the hooker, passing time. She seemed to feed on my nervousness.

"Philippines," she said, grinning wide and throwing the drapes on a single gold tooth. "My friend, he college boy, he tell me 'You know what Filipinos are? Mexicans of the East!' He Korean, so I tell him 'You know what you are? *Jews* of the East!" She gesticulated and raised her eyebrows, trying the line out on me.

"You Jew?" she cried.

"I'm an honorary Filipino. My best friend from high school is Filipino. His mom still makes me sesame chicken drumsticks whenever I come home."

I'd been ordained for a year, and when I met someone new I wasn't sure if I should give them my Zen or Christian name. That morning I'd signed a monastery fundraising letter by blurring my old signature/identity with the new one, hoping for clarity through collision.

"I'm Lavester," I said, deciding that neither name worked in this setting. "What are they calling you these days?"

I held out my hand for her to shake. She squirted hand sanitizer on it and flung the bottle back in her bag.

"You have lots of young clients?" I said.

Her face went somber, as though a parole board had materialized before her. "I work only two days a week. Part-time." She held up a pair of fingers, as though taking an oath. "Two. Days."

I sort of shrugged, unsure what kind of a reply she was cuing me for with this moral fervor for freelance hooking. *Oh, part-time.*

Does that mean you don't get dental? Well then I hope you can make the payments on that gold tooth. It'd be weird if they tried to repossess it. Most fabulous was her red-sequined dress, which was more like lingerie trying really hard to get us to think it was a dress. She was dressed up like someone who's dressed up like a prostitute. *I guess all those sorority girls at Pimps 'n' Ho's parties have been getting it right all these years.*

She clapped twice, like a wrestling referee. It was go time. My stomach dropped. I'd been making fun of her in my head because I was terrified of her. She was an assassin with my libido in her sights.

She laughed. "You so tense, dude!"

My back made a farting sound against the table as she drove her fingers into my chest. She was looking down at me. Her face was a death mask of white makeup. I was part of a ritual, unsure of who or what was being sacrificed. Backlit and haloed, you could see shock-white scalp through the frozen black whorls of hair, spun and towering like cotton candy over her furrowed brow. My grandmother on my mom's side had passed away several months before, and she'd stared back at me from her coffin with the exact same dyed-to-death space helmet of hair.

"How old are you?" I suddenly blurted out. It sounded more like an accusation than a question.

"You be old some day too!" she cried. "Look me up. I still be here!"

"Working part-time, no doubt."

Her fingers found my inner thigh and her thumb made its way down the crease where my leg ends and trouble begins. I reached out to brush my fingertips across her cheek. She gently danced backward, a move perfected through years of practice.

I had hoped that she would jump the wall of her chosen profession, as I had jumped the wall of mine; that she would meet me halfway, and when I reached out tenderly, she would accept my touch, for it was what she needed, too. I had hoped that money would be an afterthought for her, as it was for me. Like every other john, I'd floated into her world on the magic carpet of pure fantasy, which she had just yanked out from under me. I wasn't special: I was desperate. And she was going to make me pay for it.

"Eighty dollar." She rolled her tongue around in her cheek and motioned as though singing into a microphone. "Eighty dollar for with my mouth!" She opened her mouth and pointed inside.

"Yeah, yeah, I get it. The thing is, I'm so sorry, I only have sixty."

No matter what the standard, when it comes to sex, I'm bound to disappoint a woman. By now I just wanted to leave, but I've always been bad about ending a relationship once things go south.

"I take off my clothes," she said.

It was more of an old-fashioned burlesque than an erotic strip-tease. Whatever it was, it was just starting to get good when she surprised us both by getting that downsized dress stuck halfway over her head. She struggled for several seconds in a mild panic and then started spazzing out like a horsefly caught in a cobweb. Oh, how I wanted to leap to her rescue! But I was high and irrational and terrified that the ornery oldster would burst into the room just then.

What the hell's this, guy?!

It's not what you think! I cry, my hands clasped around this freaking-out woman with a dress pulled up over her head. But already he is brandishing the jerry-rigged cattle prod he keeps holstered and at the ready for unruly customers like me. Down I go in a burst of electricity, my erection jiggling in my boxers like a flagpole in a tornado.

She unsheathed herself from the cheap garment, put a hand to her hip, and tossed her hair back (it was cement, it didn't move) as if to say *I meant to do that!* Her dress floated over the lamp behind us, and the room darkened. She stepped forward. Her bra was the light bright blue of a handicap placard. She unclasped it and two enormous boobs broke free . . . and stayed there, right where they'd been told; years ago, no doubt, by a plastic surgeon—certainly not by Mother Nature, who kindly releases breasts to fall downward after they've put in a few good decades. They looked like a smile frozen on a face that had long ago forgotten what the joke was.

"Yours off now," she said.

She pointed officiously to my boxers and crossed her arms over her breasts, as if to deny access. It felt like a legal thing. I could just see that old receptionist-pimp dispensing advice with his laser pointer in the jack-shack conference room as bored Asian call girls texted each other behind his back.

You can get off on the hooker's version of entrapment IF?

And they in monotonous unison: *Office Scumbag takes off his undies himself.*

Amen sisters, keep them hands off the Hanes!

I slipped out of my boxers and was naked for the first time in three years in front of someone who wasn't a bald flabby monk dragging his saggy gray balls into a shower stall. She was naked too—save those flesh-toned pantyhose.

Flesh-toned hose!? She had copper C-3PO legs.

We quietly regarded each other for a moment, this oldest member of the world's oldest profession and her lonely monastic charge. Beauty doesn't charm me. Humanity does. And she was all human, standing there with half a smile and one gold tooth, this knowing mockery of a striptease over half a century old.

"Can I touch you?" I asked.

There are winds inside you, winds as powerful as the ones outside you. Sometimes these inner winds are stronger than your will to control them, and they tear away at your resistance, like the Santa Ana winds that stripped those shingles, one by one, off the sutrahall roof that evening. If you're still here with me, perhaps at one time you have been blown by the same winds that blew through me that night. Perhaps, like me, you have huddled against these winds with the wrong person.

With one fluid motion she outfitted the pole upon which I'd vaulted over the wall that evening with a bright maroon condom.

It lay there, red and slightly curved, like the thumb of a hitchhiker begging for a ride. The latex was heavy and thick. It felt like a rubber mask, as though I were robbing a bank from the waist down. She put the "little red bandit" in her mouth and began bobbing up and down with methodical precision, like an oil rig.

I'd forgotten how weird sexual intimacy with a stranger can be. I sort of hovered over my body, embarrassed, as though someone was wiping my butt for me. Surely what she lacked in youth she made up for with experience, dazzling me with an astonishing array of techniques, right?

She had no idea what she was doing.

Or, if she had an idea, it was the wrong one, but after decades spent mastering this full-blown oral error, she was sticking to it. She took me way too deeply into her mouth, and made gagging noises, like a cat coughing up a hairball. I didn't know whether to enjoy myself or perform the Heimlich maneuver.

She was bent over me, curved into a slick-bodied L, her ass arched upward like a cat that's just landed on its feet. I reached toward her pivot point, a dark squiggle of unshaved heat. I closed my eyes and put my hand against her. Warm, wet, an expression of pure softness: I felt sweet breath whispering from inside her, calling my name ... *Lavester!*

As earthly as this opening is to its owner, it is equally God-like to a lost and lonely man. It felt like I was fondling the slit to her soul. I rested my fingers there. But my fingers fell inward, slid inside, perfectly encased and allowed, the opening accepting—meeting—my touch, pulling me in ... and in ... and in.

I reached a long way inside her. .... If I'd had a free hand, I would have called time-out.

I could not find the actual hole. I'm not making this up. Women: I have been, give or take, with twenty of you, and every last one of you has been shaped as though by the hand of your very own Michelangelo; and the hand that explores you for the first time, feeling the masterpiece between your legs, lost and found all at once, always has to learn your special grooves all over again. Can you see why we men fuck up our lives, and yours, again and again, just to shake hands with what's inside you? That's why I've taken you over the wall and up inside my boo, so you can feel this too, what it feels like inside of you.

In any event, she had no hole. I slid my fingers back and back . . . but there was no going up and in. I was heading anus-ward fast.

She had a shamgina!

Then my fingers disappeared through "the roof." There was an astonishing pool of upside-down wetness waiting for me. It was weird. The way she'd rolled her hips back made it difficult to find an opening into her last bit of privacy. But find it I did. She moaned. I grinned: *Makin' momma proud!*

A lot can run through a guy's head during moments like this. Here's what ran through mine: *She's not wet from me—this is from a previous job. Which means it's either lube. OR . . .* But I couldn't tell. Couldn't tell if her crescendoing gasps were fake or if she was actually enjoying herself. But if this was all an act, well, at least she really seemed to be enjoying faking it, which is about all you can ask for in a situation like this. I worked my hips, joining her rhythm, sliding myself from the back of her throat to the front of her mouth—which fastened and held me there, her lips moving quickly, gripping tight. The bones in my hips began to melt; my stomach dropped through the floor; a ball of gentle fire proceeded to rumble from my core—white hot light—my jaw flung open, nearly dislocated, like a magical beast leaving its body through its mouth, and I released everything I had, a body filled to bursting, into the red rubber mask.

Like I said, it had been a while.

She gently guided me back down, decreasing pressure, lips tapering off, smoothing my quivery reentry into the room . . . my place on the massage table . . . my breath, in that blank-walled box. I remember her smoothly intercepting my hand, at which point I realized—as she had, an instant earlier—that I was unconsciously raising my fingers to my nostrils. I wanted to smell her. Hand sanitizer and a washcloth at the ready, she removed all traces of herself from me. There was nothing left of her when I put my fingers to my nose, just stinging fresh alcohol. She removed the condom and gently took the grease and puddle away, like a distracted mother wiping her baby's bottom.

Traffic bleated and purred outside. I was still very much on planet earth. The whole world had not stopped in its tracks and put a hand to its mouth just because I'd done something naughty. I had sinned, but the mechanisms of existence had not blinked. We could amend Hannah Arendt's phrase "banality of evil" to "banality of ego." Life goes on, directing back upon you all of the energies and actions you have put out there. This is karma. A great wave of lust had issued from me, and to me and me alone it returned. How could it be any other way? Sexual acts have consequences. Babies, HIV, heartbreak, love—or nothing at all. Hollow nausea, as though something had been removed from inside me and my organs lay hot against the emptiness.

I watched her colossal, stiff breasts sway like the twin heads of two great farm animals. They looked oxymoronic on her, like a soccer uniform on a senior citizen. And isn't that always how it goes? Those same qualities that seem so attractive in the heat of the moment look slightly foreign and out of place afterward. This can be endearing with someone you care about. But with someone you hardly know?

"Where you from?" she asked.

"Uptown," I lied.

"Uptown?—*hoo, hoo, hoo.*" She kicked her naked leg up on the massage table and stretched her hamstrings.

"You come all the way here from Uptown?"

"I was in the neighborhood canvassing for a political cause."

I could just see us monks chanting in the sutra hall when she bursts through the double doors in that doily of a dress and flesh-toned hose: "It's BJ time, dudes!" I didn't want her knowing anything about me. I'm not sure why, then, unprompted and out of nowhere, I suddenly told her the truth.

"I was scared to come here this evening."

"How come scared?"

"I don't know, this is new to me."

"Next time easier." She nodded. "Next time easier."

Will there be a next time? There I am, a washed-up Zen master, banging on the brothel door with a malt-liquor bottle. "I have deep insight into the non-dual nature of our universe!" I cry, offering the only currency I have. "Yes, but you're a sexist, shallow little shit of a human being!" comes her reply from inside, where she is high-fiving my inner Ethel. "So what good is it?"

My single-serving sex partner stood before me like a kid waiting for her allowance. I opened my wallet and gave her everything. Two twenties, a pair of fives, two ones—eight bucks shy of our agreed upon price, which did not go unnoticed. How would I explain it to my fellow monks when, in lieu of full payment, Mr. Roper the Pimp broke both my thumbs?

What could she do? Her tits sagged sadly. I lowered my open wallet and her eyes shot to the six C-notes therein.

"That's not mine," I cried. "That belongs to someone else. It really does, I swear to God."

"Your wife?"

"No! My teacher."

"You in school? Why you have teacher's money?"

"It's a gift. It's a gift for him."

"Gift for him, nothing for me?"

I scrambled through my wallet and produced a Barnes & Noble gift card my librarian aunt had given me. "This has at least fifteen bucks on it. Here, it's yours!"

She stared at me with half a smile, nodding her head a little, like a fighter coming to understand an opponent. She took the gift card and my wallet, put the gift card back in the wallet, and handed me the wallet. Then she carefully laid the money I'd given her on the massage table and removed her shiny red dress from the lamp. Light flooded the room. She slid the dress over her head, sequins crackling, gyrated and jiggled her hips and shoulders, writhed and danced, but could not get into the thing herself.

"Bro?!" cried a voice from under the fabric.

I slipped my hands under the hem of the dress, stalled at her armpits, and gently tugged.

"You tear this fabric I'm gonna kill you."

I lowered the garment past her breasts, ribs, belly button, and gave it a sharp tug over her ass. I was on my knees, and she was staring down at me. I stood up and she moved uncomfortably close, as though trying to intimidate me. Then she reached down and put her hand against my zipper. I considered giving her all six hundred of my teacher's dollars, jumping the monastery wall, and never looking back.

"You gonna have to come back. You still owe me. Okay?"

"Okay. I'll be back."

"I mean it. You owe me."

"I know. I know. I'll be back."

She tucked the money into her dress, a big wad of crumbly cash fanning out from her cleavage. She looked more like a bookie than a hooker. She looked cute. She was the kind of person who did things that she thought she was supposed to do to be sexy, which somehow made her a parody of sexy, and sexy, at the same time.

I couldn't believe it. I was hard all over again. And I'm hard now thinking about it. You can beat yourself to within an inch of your life out of sexual guilt, but lying in your hospital bed, bloody and wheezing, you will get an erection when a curvy nurse comes to wipe the shit off your thighs. You have to do the right thing, only you're not built to: such is the koan of living in a body—male, in my case. My inner Ethel is not the answer. Nor is an erotic masseuse. But what the answer is, I don't know.

I do know this: I never went back. There was no real feeling between us—just stimulation. I wrote a check with my dick that my heart couldn't cash, and I felt like a cheat afterward. Every day, monks the world over display heroic feats of willpower by resisting their grosser desires, but they often remain ignorant of their most basic human needs. It's the occupational hazard of a renunciate. I refused any female contact for three years, and then I completely broke down and face-fucked a hooker. Which raises the question: Is there a middle way between maintaining a strong spiritual discipline and being honest about your needs? If you become attached to your role as someone who has left the world and its pleasures behind, then when your body, your life, cries out in hunger, you will feed it poison to try and shut it up, as though it was crying out for poison in the first place.

I did not wake up that morning thinking *Today I will be a human animal, not a human being.* It just happened. Surely there were warning signs along the way. Why didn't I listen? Was I more interested in power than growth, in taking control of the monastery than in taking responsibility for it? Was I searching for my true self, or for the identity and status that had eluded me all those years I stumbled around in the world trying to find my place?

Was I happy?

Lonely?

God, I was lonely.

She was paid up, and the stretch of silence meant it was time for me to go. I paused in the doorway. We still had one unfinished piece of business. "What's your name?" I asked for the second time that evening.

She thought about it for a moment ... "Sue!"

I wondered if she had momentarily thought of her real name and then decided to give me her fake hooker name, or if she had first thought of her fake hooker name and then decided to give me her real name. I hoped that Sue was true—I wanted something real to take with me when I jumped back over the wall. Underneath all carnal desire is a wish to know the world, to claim it not *for* yourself, but *as* yourself. Sometimes, a bad mistake, consciously made, can teach you this better than a good rule unconsciously followed. You learn that the world will not give itself freely to you until you give yourself freely to it. This is the true love that we seek through our flawed and fleshy fumblings; it is what we are looking for when we jump the wall.

Ultimately, the Way is not straightforward, it's like GPS—you take a wrong turn and it immediately recalibrates based on your mistake. I've always felt that at some point all the dead ends you've taken in life converge, and you find yourself at a crossroads with no doubt about which path to take. You've taken them all by now, and you know they all lead to the same place, by more or less direct routes. It's comforting to remember this during those moments when I feel the most lost and alone.

"Goodbye, Lavester," Sue said, flashing that golden tooth and shutting the door between us.

5

Consider the Seed

It is the size of a pea, and crisp green. Feel it in your fingers: the packed potential within its smooth borders; the tight, pinprick tip—that searching extension of sentience. Put it into the earth with me. Black mineral loam, juicy, flecked with bits of organic energy; arms from underground, waiting for our baby seed. Let's spend a few weeks with it underground. Plant the seed in your imagination. Earth presses up against it; caressing it . . . it draws the earth into itself. The soil offers its minerals to the seed. Seed and soil flowing into one another.

A fundamental law of nature: for the right mate, all precincts are porous. Moisture pierces the seed's green skin, much to its joy. Sun bakes through the soil, heats the love inside our seed. Carbon dioxide from the air clicks into another mode inside the seed, wakes up newly when it wanders within and meets the family of factors gathered there. Who's in charge here? Is the seed co-opting its environment? Is the outside world invading the world inside our seed? There is a party going on inside there. An orgy. Nobody knows any better. All of nature is naked inside that seed; elements are uniting, reconfiguring, something new is arising.

It's all coming together—upside down and inside out.

The seed can be looked at in and of itself. Or it can be seen as a point in a process. Sitting quietly, breathing, inside and outside interpenetrating, we come up against similar wonderings. Where does one thing end and another begin? Contemplation involves slowing the mind down, taking it into the breath, until it manifests the natural rhythms of life itself, and no longer needs to grasp at the fruit of mental energy; you are down in the soil where thoughts grow, arise, die away. The foundation. The source. Giving rise to the ten thousand things, the whole manifest universe. I often contemplate the seed of our cosmos, which scientists tell us was very small and dense and hot: we were all packed in there together back in the day. Our minds and bank accounts and families were fused as one. Then there was an explosion, and we were torn apart. Our basic DNA is stardust, cosmologists tell us. We then grew arms and eardrums to connect once again. Blood gurgled up to lubricate our movements. We grew feet to walk toward each other; retinas to take each other in; fingers to pick lice from each others' coats of hair, and to slide rings onto one another.

We are designed to come back together once more, and we all exploded outward way back when so that we could begin the long, slow climb back into each other's arms. Without distance, without being apart, we could never then become one. If we were still packed together in that infinitesimally dense cosmic seed, where your lung was my hand and my thoughts were your blood, we could never bear witness to oneness, which is a beautiful thing and deserves an audience. Things flow into each other and back to themselves, gaining themselves through the other and the other through themselves. It's natural. Everything falls into its proper place after spending some time apart. "We just fit together," a girlfriend told me years ago. "It's perfect." We had just made love, which is to say we had forgotten ourselves by way of each other, as only two young souls filled to bursting with themselves can.

Recently, I spent some time with a tiny baby girl, and this was her process: She touched her surroundings with her eyes, blinking often to clear the way for more receiving. She used her chubby fingers to grope the air and pat-pat-pat the wooden floor. She pivoted on her squat little butt, an empress, the earth beneath her, her throne. She produced sounds that filled our ears. It was the sound of a seed pushing through soil. She grew very fast, before our eyes, in just a couple of hours. Along the way she often became fed up with this process and started sobbing.

Enough already! I'd like to stay the same, if you don't mind! I'd rather not have to grow up!

But, of course, not growing up is not an option. You have to grow, little girl. It's what you do. So the tears come, the agony of arising. Growing pains. The tears and trembles wash and shake her clean. Into her mother's arms she goes, and we all turn back to each other and share adult conversation and go to the bathroom and sip our black tea, and then ten minutes later, there she is back on the bamboo floor again, lips damp and belly bubbling with breast milk. Only she is a little older now. Dead from a few minutes before, and reborn. Extending a little further out of herself, finding fresh faces to explore, reaching out and touching, fiddling with our lips, like a harpist plucking song from strings. Digesting something new from her surroundings, she turns it into the food of experience, and then interacts in a fresh way with her surroundings.

We laugh our asses off. We call this "playing."

What I won't forget are her big, global eyes, swirling white and sapphire and fresh from tears, as teeming and tight as the tiny green seed.

I lived at a Zen Buddhist monastery for a decade, and here's what I learned to have faith in: Outside of me, there is a perfect home for everything inside of me. And inside of me, there is a perfect home for everything outside of me. Just let it go, and let it in. In and out, like the breath. After all, outside has nowhere to go but in, and inside has nowhere to go but out. My job, our job, is to broker the exchange between the two, to manifest the interpenetration of inside and outside, of self and other. That's all. I dissolve in activity, in relationship with my surroundings, so that the inner world can flow out, and the outer world can arrive within. I have to both put in effort and know when to let go. There's a natural balance, a dance, between embracing and releasing: turning your surroundings into yourself, like the tree that absorbs carbon dioxide, and turning yourself into your surroundings, like the same tree releasing oxygen.

This is what Buddhists call the Middle Way.

I am sometimes asked how I've changed in my career as a full-time Zen monk. Often the question is pretty pointed. Young students want to know what they're getting into. Before taking up Zen, I was like a seed that, upon being introduced to minerals, water, oxygen, and sunlight, says something like, "Oh no, thank you, but I'd rather not have you permeate my borders and transform me from within. That's a little much. I have my boundaries. I don't want to let the world in. And I surely don't want to release the best part of myself back to the world. I'm a seed, after all. I want to become a *bigger* seed, you see, not a plant or a bush or a mulberry tree."

Yet my very cells, stacked and hollow, ached for input; and the wiggle and flow within pressed against my borders for release. I needed to grow. Hunched, scowling, unsure of everything, I walked around like a question mark, which, if you think about it, looks like half of a heart too firmly upright. Slant a little! Slide into the arms of the world around you! Meet your match, which is always coming from the other way!

What's the best part of you? Your heart. What happens if you don't feed it? It grumbles and, like an empty stomach, eats away at you. Do you imagine that the rest of you doesn't operate on the exact same principle as the best part of you? Your very being, all its parts, and the sum of you that is greater than those parts, amount to nothing more than unrequited love, an open womb, soft earth, into which your surroundings plant seeds, so that your fulfillment gradually manifests as seeds that fit perfectly with your surroundings. As our environment cultivates us, we cultivate our environment.

When we sit *zazen,* or Zen meditation, we manifest oneness with our surroundings. We don't go anywhere or do anything. We don't take flights of mental fancy or work ourselves into a spiritual fervor. We sink down in our seat. We don't wear earplugs. And we keep our eyes open, with a soft gaze. Our spines are straight, our minds are clear, our hearts are open. Our whole body comes alive through stillness. Our belly button is a third eye, opening and closing with each breath. Once upon a time, a root, a blood-filled branch, extended from our mother into this third eye, and it still tingles with awareness for the world around us.

"Where are you when you see the flower?" Roshi would ask, over and over, during *sanzen,* our private koan meetings.

I would turn to the vase of flowers and furrow my brow, waiting for an answer. Those flowers were implacable: their petals were practically crossed, like a pair of arms. They didn't budge. *I'm over here and they're over there,* my mind concluded. *And never the twain shall meet.*

One day, when, for whatever reason, I didn't get a chance to think about it, I took the flowers in, and smiled. I bloomed along with the flowers. How the flowers went from that vase to my lips is a miracle. Let me unpack the miracle: I realized that the life in the flowers and the life in me *are the same life.* We are two halves of one experience. The flowers took root within me and blossomed, because we were never fundamentally separate. We were within each other all along. We occupy one cosmos together.

We are never more than a breath away from the home we share with the entire universe. Zazen meditation is just us checking back in. "Hi Honey, I'm home; Hi Honey, I'm home," over and over. We are still hugged together as closely as we were back in the days of the cosmic seed. Nothing can be added to or subtracted from an already complete universe. The energy that once held us tight hasn't gone anywhere. When the universe exploded outward, it had nowhere to go but back into itself.

So why bother separating in the first place? we sometimes ask, struggling to hold down our corner of the cosmos in the meditation hall.

And sometimes the universe answers: *I needed to give myself some room to breathe. But don't worry, in the blink of an eye we'll all be back together again.*

During these moments, we often wish the universe had kept its big fat mouth shut. We don't like being reminded of the reunion that awaits us. We're designed to fall in love with our short time on this planet, where there is room enough for all of us to breathe.

When I first moved to the monastery, I hated it. I didn't get it. I felt its goodness, sure—my bones knew I was in the right place, but my mind was like, *Get me the hell out of here!* The environment was trying to work on me, to get in there, the way soil works on a seed. I preferred to stay young and green. Seed-wise, I wanted to stay in my packet. I didn't want to grow. I spent my days off in the computer room, visiting a website I like to call evilzen.com. I read essay after essay about how corrupt and backward American Zen Buddhist practice had become. I loved it. It hit the spot, all this negativity. At one point I contacted the owner of the website, and we began a correspondence. He urged me to leave the monastery.

"Get on with your life! You're running away from reality up on that mountain!" he said.

I took his words to heart, but my heart was strangely unmoved. I'd planted my roots in that mountain soil, and I couldn't seem to budge. I talked a lot, to anyone who would listen, about leaving, but every morning I woke up at four, scuttled off to the zendo, and sat and breathed.

One day I repaired to the tech cabin, booted up the student computer, waited several hours for the infernally archaic machine to finally produce a web browser, and went to type in evilzen.com. That's when my jaw went slack and fell to the snow-wet carpet and stayed there. This was in 2004, a day after Christmas. A tsunami had hit Southeast Asia. I remember the figure: 283,000 dead. A massive sinkhole of meaning and hope had opened up halfway around the world. I sat there for a very long time becoming acquainted with the horror through photos. A gray dog with no discernible head washed up against someone's home. Grandmothers, children, mustached men, and wild-haired wives—photo after photo . . . click, click, click . . . everyone with the same expression, mouths and eyes circular, just screaming and screaming in agony.

I remember thinking three things, and scribbling them in my journal, reproduced here:

1. My worries here on the mountaintop are insignificant in comparison to what 90 percent of what humanity has to deal with. Do the words QUALITY PROBLEMS mean anything to you, white boy?
2. One sentence: *Life is not fair.*
3. If you leave this mountaintop, you will not escape. Whatever you're running from you will face again in whatever you are running to. You cannot escape the human condition.

And this is where it gets hard. Everyone understands that a seed must let the world in so that it can grow, and truth be told, the seed doesn't seem to mind. And everyone more or less gets that the baby's tears water its own little green shoots and roots; pain is part of her growing process. "There there," we say, burping her on our shoulder. "It's okay." When it comes to babies and seeds, we get it. No problem. But what about when the same natural process that gives rise to and nurtures us destroys us indiscriminately, brutally, violently? What about when our daughters are raped, our jobs are lost, our cars crash, and our brain chemicals go haywire? What about when our surroundings turn on us, and swallow us whole, like the ocean that swallowed those 283,000 people?

I don't believe in spirits, but that doesn't mean they're not out there. Ten years ago, when a mechanism lowered my grandmother's shiny black casket into the earth—*click, click, click*—my thirty-year-old cousin started sobbing. This set off a chain reaction, and all ten of my little nieces and nephews joined in. Their tears watered the air, brought it alive. I swear I heard my grandmother's voice then: "*Life is precious because it ends. If it went on and on and on forever, it would be very cheap indeed.*" Spoken like a true Depression-era baby, who knew the value of things, and even repurposed every last piece of junk mail as scrap paper.

Her final days were not entirely pretty, and I often contemplate them on the cushion. She became incontinent. There was shit smeared on most of the chairs in her apartment, where she lived alone. Apparently, she ate only bite-size candy bars those final few weeks of her life. When my mother arrived after getting the call, and saw her mother's dead body, she screamed and screamed for a Catholic priest. Something shorted inside her head, and she lost all but 30 percent of her hearing in one ear.

It's easy to understand what a seed or a baby is going through, but it's hard to extend our appreciation to the corpses of loved ones. Life is precious. We hate to see it go. But if it went on and on, ours would be a horrible universe. There would be infinite darkness into and from which our lives grew and grew. We would become impossibly ancient, losing all sensitivity; we would no longer be able to feel love, or taste food, like my grandma, who in the end subsisted simply on sugar highs. We would be like those Guinness World Record holders who grow their fingernails out into dense, gnarled, tortuous tree roots—only not just our fingernails but every aspect of our selves would spread, swell, twist in on us in unruly patterns, making the simplest daily rituals a hellish nightmare. I would take up smoking again, and smoke and smoke and smoke, spending whole centuries under a bridge, smoking and masturbating and picking off sewer rats with a handgun. I certainly wouldn't do anything good with my interminable life. What would be the point?

Where there is no death (and there is nowhere where there is no death, except maybe vampire novels), there are no risks, and life is utterly meaningless.

Life is precious, and so death must be precious too. Our job is to figure out why. So we sit on our cushions and breathe. One breath ends, the next begins. We sink down into the earth, where the inhale and the exhale meet—head into each other—exchange positions, dying over and over for each other: giving life to us, like the seed that dies in order to become a tree. We're dying and being reborn every instant of our lives—blink, and your twenty-first birthday becomes your seventieth, your dimples now wrinkles, your face a map of everywhere you've been and all you've done in that blink of an eye.

One experience ends, the next begins, but nothing really changes. We're still packed inside that cosmic seed. We simply have a little more room to breathe. But don't worry: we're coming back together. Each day, we're getting closer and closer to the source, and each other. Try to not be afraid, and I'll try along with you. Let's practice the dark celebration of mourning, and release, on the cushion and in our lives. We are part of a process, and eventually the momentum, like the inhale or exhale, will shift the other way. Perhaps death is merely the negative image, or reverse process, of life. The same thing heading the opposite way. One universe differently emphasized.

As I finish this, the sun is setting, which means it's rising somewhere else. A jet is gurgling across the sky, going from here to there, and back again. Snow floats down from that same sky, where it will return once more with the spring thaw. Everything is as it should be—except for me, and maybe you.

But don't worry, we're getting there too.

6

A Treaty of Love

When I met Leonard Cohen, I was a failed writer, and I acted like one. We were waiting to bow into the walking meditation line at our head temple in LA. I pretended I didn't know who he was and asked him if my Ford Festiva was parked in the right place.

"Sure," he said.

I feigned surprise: "'Everybody Knows.' I'd recognize that voice anywhere."

His monk's name, Jikan, means "noble silence," and he manifested it then. I was mortified.

I gave up writing to become a Zen monk, and then, a decade after meeting Jikan, I wrote a book about being a monk. Lizzie, Roshi's *inji*, or attendant, served as a proxy for my ambition and left chapters of the work-in-progress in his cabin during a retreat. By then I was the head monk at the monastery, and I approached Jikan at the end of a long day to ask how his back was. He was short, thin, and old, but he still sat like a rock in the zendo.

"I don't feel a thing," he said.

I nodded: "Your meditation must be really strong."

He shook his head and said, "OxyContin." Then he looked into my eyes with a clear, almost startled expression: "Hey, I love your book. How can I help?" I refused all his generous offers but one, and he wrote the book's foreword.

He had a decades-long relationship with Roshi, and it was my privilege to witness these two powerful men "make relationship," as Roshi would say.

I think Roshi liked having Jikan around because Jikan did not make any demands on him. They could just sip tea in silence. (Once people start talking, they inevitably start fighting, Roshi said.)

One afternoon, Roshi, 106 years old by then, diminished by both age and the sex scandal that devastated our community and his reputation, had a massive accident in his adult diapers. As I took Roshi to the bathroom, Jikan filled a basin with warm water, removed his suit coat and cuff links, and rolled up his crisp white sleeves.

"Jikan, I can do that part," I said.

"I wouldn't think of it," he said.

I helped Roshi stand while Jikan knelt behind him and gently wiped him clean.

Watching Jikan serve our teacher, unobsequiously and with intelligence, care, and respect, helped take the sting out of my own failures as a writer and as a man. You learn that there is something greater than artistic success when you see a great artist humbling himself before it. Jikan, like any good monk, was devoted to what his teacher was devoted to.

He and Roshi had a similar project, a shared vision: Roshi taught it, Leonard sang it. With none of Leonard's eloquence or Roshi's wisdom at my disposal, I would describe it as the union of contrary things—and then their separation again, and the struggle in between.

In different ways, they each gave their lives to breaking and maintaining silence on what Buddhists call the Great Matter and what Roshi called True Love. Was Leonard an artist consumed by despair? No, his work was shot through with the opposite of despair. But in Leonard's world, the opposite of despair was not hope—it was clarity. From this clarity came the vision of a prophet: "I've seen the future, brother / It is murder."

Jikan wasn't just a visionary artist. He was a profoundly generous man. When Roshi became grievously ill, Jikan visited every day, month after month, bringing Lizzie and me food, gifts, and his inimitable company. One night he told me a hilarious and risqué story involving him and a Zen nun. I didn't know him very well at that point. I thought, "Why is he telling me this? He knows I'm a writer with few qualms about publishing personal stuff. He must know I'm going to use this!" Then I caught something in his face—though I think he'd caught something in mine, first. There was a moment of silence. I wondered if he would continue speaking. He searched inside himself for more details, and kept sharing.

That's when I got it: *He's giving me material.*

That's what I mean by generous.

The penultimate time I saw Jikan, I was getting lunch on Larchmont Street with an old friend from my Hollywood screenwriting days. I had given him a copy of my book. Only one thing about it impressed him: "Dude, I can't believe you know Leonard Cohen!"

We left the pizza parlor, turned the corner, and who should be sitting at a table outside a burger restaurant but Jikan Leonard Cohen himself. His "Stranger Music" office was nearby, and we spent the afternoon brainstorming about how to revitalize the monastery now that our teacher was dead.

"What if you put in a rifle range and get a bunch of young guys up there?" Jikan said. "Man, if I were fifteen minutes younger, I'd join you."

Yes, rifles. For all the self-satisfied liberals who want to claim him as one of their own, I'm sorry, but Leonard Cohen belongs to everyone. Once, when we were waiting in the lobby at the doctor's office, he said: "My National Rifle Association hat came in the mail today. I looked at the tag. I couldn't believe it: Made in China!"

After I rearranged my jaw on my face from its descent to the floor, I said, "You're an N.R.A. member?"

He kept staring straight ahead. "Let's keep that between us," he said.

I think of that episode now, during our current historical moment. I have no idea how Jikan would have voted in the past presidential election, but if there was anyone who could hold both extremes in his hand and heart, it was the man who, for the last words on his last album, chose these: "I wish there was a treaty we could sign / . . . I wish there was a treaty between your love and mine."

For an artist informed by a vision of True Love, opposite forces and peoples are just different kinds of love trying to meet. Jikan sang of and from the longing in this struggle.

The last time I saw him, he looked epiphanic and light, as if he were disappearing. There was great pain in his eyes, and his breath was heavy.

He told me that during his stay in India after his years at our Zen monastery, something clicked and he found a peace inside that had never left him. "This stuff works," he said. "Somehow everything I've been doing all these years comes down to the work I did with Roshi."

He played his new album for me. At the end, gorgeous, soft strings set the tone, lulling you into a drifting, pensive melancholy. Then his voice emerges with the wish for a treaty of love. He sat in silence before me, this aged, tiny, impeccably dressed poet, his black fedora tilted lightly on his head, his voice booming all around us.

When I heard those final lines, it was like he split me open with a ray of light. My face grew hot, my heart pounded. I was sobbing inside. I knew he was saying goodbye to all of us.

I miss you, beloved brother monk and mentor. The world needs spiritual artists now more than ever. We need artists who are afraid of something other than their own failure, who bow down before something greater than likes, legacy, and culture creation.

In a world filled with climbers, fakes, and opportunists, from our street corners and churches all the way to Washington, D.C., you were the real deal. You alone could give voice to these dark times, but when I call your name there is only noble silence.

7

Expiration Date

A human being has a shelf life. It's a strange thought, given how essential we tend to think we are, as though we'll be around forever. But no. We're born, we ripen, we die. And how do we die? I was on my knees, boxer shorts around an ankle, not only praying but vomiting, and not only vomiting but battling ferocious incontinence, when I realized, *We all die like dogs.*

When I had no more food left in me, I heaved up a semen-looking fluid, some sort of digestive ectoplasm. Now I was puking nothing but hot wind, and I was puking it with such force that it felt like my skull was changing its shape.

Not that the situation was without humor. Kuru, the monastery cat, kept poking his black nose around the bathroom door behind me. This afforded him the perfect view of my naked posterior. He was a rescue cat, and I'd nursed him to life in front of a furnace. The first thing he did upon regaining his strength was bite my nose. We'd been loving, antagonistic playmates ever since. He took this opportunity to get the best of me. In a cruel mockery of our usual routine, where I dangled a cloth mouse on a rope and he had at it, I saw a blur of fur and felt a sting between my legs. He was batting my testicles with his claw.

"Kuuuru!" I cried, like Marlon Brando blubbering "Stell-llah!" He darted behind the sink as I lamely tried to kill him with my foot. Then he lunged for me again as I gasped and retched in the toilet. He began beating my balls like a boxer working a speed bag.

I sobbed. *We all die like dogs.*

The monastery was empty, which suited me. I like to suffer alone. The other monks were on retreat in LA, but I'd stayed behind to watch camp. An hour earlier I'd awoken with a sting in the left side of my abdomen, as though I'd swallowed a fishhook and someone was tugging the line. It felt like a communication from the land of the dead. After another hour of vomiting, then spinning around, sitting, and shitting, vomiting and shitting, vomiting and shitting, I felt my hands start tingling and my eyes go fuzzy, almost carbonated: I saw stars. Each hellburst of vomitiarrhea built upon the last in strength and duration, like a sick parody of the womb contractions that swell into childbirth. I lapsed into a semiconscious state as the rising sun warmed the walls. I had the strangest feeling that my body was pregnant with its antithesis, as though a howling death baby was clawing its way out of me.

The only thing that could hurt this much, in just this way, is giving birth, I thought. *Or dying.*

I fell to the carpet before the toilet and just began to wail. I rested my head on my clenched fists and screamed, "Please God please God please God." But you cannot pray your way around what God has placed squarely in your path. So I called 911. I was huddled in a death clump in the room where Roshi gives private koan interviews when the paramedics stormed the cabin.

"I think I have food poisoning," I said.

The tall, sinewy one from the fire department produced a silver tube of activated charcoal. He had a sweet expression and trustworthy eyes.

"Will that make me throw up?" I asked.

"Nope."

"Are you just saying that?"

"No sir, we don't do that."

I sucked down some of the thick paste and instantly scream-puked all over the wall and carpet and a row of my teacher's robes, which were hanging in plastic dry-cleaning bags.

"We're going to take you to the hospital," he said.

Moments later I was staring at the ambulance ceiling. A big strong woman put a blanket over me, tastefully covering my dick, which was hanging out of my boxers, sloping to one side like an exhausted gerbil. She kept asking, "You okay?" When I was not, she would hold open a plastic bag, I would tilt my head, and more horrible wonders would pour out of my mouth. In this way, we inched down the mountain switchbacks. I was being escorted not only to the hospital, but to a whole new frame of mind. I was about to become a "patient," which is a telling term.

Patience is key to your mental health when you are physically ill. It is one of the few virtues you can actively cultivate when your body ceases to cooperate. When sick, you must practice the lost art of waiting and seeing, for your life is now on hold. You must slow down to meet the rhythms of a body that is fighting with itself, for you. The problem is, once you do slow down, the demons—the anxieties and fears you were fleeing while you were healthy—finally catch up with you. Now, when you are at your lowest, they swarm over you and feast on you, like those African ants that devour a wildebeest from hoof to horn—a black stream rushing over heaving flesh, washing away the meat, organs, entrails, leaving nothing but gleaming white bone.

Sickness ravishes you spiritually and strips you to the bone.

The emergency room was the kind of place that makes you believe in hell, but not God. Freckled children in hospital gowns; weeping immigrants; a husband wearing his wife's blood. *How can the walls of this place keep from melting?* All the surfaces were lined with hard tile so that blood and guts could be easily hosed down the floor drains. Nurses wheeled my gurney behind a plastic curtain. I wasn't sure whom I belonged to. Several medical professionals poked me and took my information, but everyone seemed to have someplace else to be. They kept asking for my Social Security number, which served to remind me that I was incurring expenses that would be somewhere in between the price of a nice used car and a commercial flight to outer space. I began making up numbers.

"Six six six, six six nine, six nine six nine."

"That's an odd number!"

"*BLAAAAA*"—and again I vomited into a plastic bag.

"Nurse, nurse, please help me! Please please, Ay yiy yiy!" a Mexican woman screamed from the other side of my curtain.

A doctor parted the curtain, clutching my blood test. What I learned was this: "Your lipase and amylase levels are through the roof."

Welcome to amylase and lipase.

"What's that mean?" I asked.

She gave a detailed and thorough answer that told me nothing.

The Mexican woman continued to wail: "Oh please give me something! Ay yiy yiy! Oh please God God God!"

"Whus rung with her?" I asked. My lips felt like rubber.

A nurse's aide turned to me: "Absolutely nothing! She's doing great!"

All forty-three muscles in his face slid into place as he smiled. I was smiling too. Something new was trickling through the IV in my arm: Dilaudid, an esteemed member of the morphine family. Everything became like an opium dream. Slow and creamy. Even the stock-still silver instruments were dancing a little. There was still pain, yes, but not *my* pain—it was as though a horrible battle was coming to a head several miles beneath me. Not my problem. Good luck with that, guys.

I want to say that when they wheeled the screaming Mexican woman past my curtain our eyes met, and something was exchanged, but what I really remember is the period of relative calm that followed her departure. Then a new nurse was sitting on the gurney beside me. Her lips were blood red and collagen-puffed into a kind of permanent "Why me?" grimace. Her makeup looked like a second face, both masking and magnifying the one underneath. Such a strange sight, this giver of care! Somewhere in between a shaman and a stripper.

"With enzyme levels like this, it's probably pancreatic cancer," she began. "I think you probably have this cancer . . . yeah. It's not uncommon. Pavarotti just died from it. You know, the opera singer? It's usually irreversible," she said. "It's inoperable," she added, in case I had missed that.

"You die from it?"

"You die from it. Generally. Yeah. But we'll let you know for sure," she said, and then she nodded solemnly and left the room.

I want to slow the story down here, because this is where time *really* slowed for me, slowed until it stopped cold at the very beginning of what appeared to be the very end of my life. I could almost feel the Great Wheels of Existence grinding to a halt all around me. I entered a time that was entirely within myself, stared through the rustling curtain into the busyness beyond, and took the situation in.

Speeding gurneys, blinking lights, worried brows. I could hear and feel my breath, but nothing else. It was about 10:00 a.m. For the first time that day I was not afraid, and for this I thank the combination of my first real taste of death and my first real opium high. The pain made me lucid, the drug made me dreamy: and so I had a kind of lucid dream, a vision.

Everyone carries their death within them, I thought. *And this is the death that I've been carrying within me. Cancer.*

My whole life I had been looking forward to something. And now it hit me like the wake-up slap on a newborn's behind—it was almost comical: *What the hell have I been looking forward to?*

Except the end. That's what comes next. The future is the finish line. That's what's finally waiting for us around the next corner.

But here's the interesting thing: I felt absolutely no regret. I didn't feel that I had missed a single thing in my life or done a single thing that I should not have done. I realized that my life itself was the only standard by which my life could be judged, and therefore it had been, in its own way, perfect. A conclusion is what gives the preceding events coherence and meaning, and now that I knew how it would end, there was nothing about my life that I would have changed. It was like a wife I had been on uneasy terms with for decades, but in this moment I came to realize that I was in love with every little thing about her, and I had been all along.

A shadow came over me. A kind but grim-faced doctor was standing there, blocking the overhead light.

He said, "You have pancreatitis."

"I know." I figured this was the name of my little cancer baby. "How long do I have left?"

He laughed without smiling. "You've already survived the worst of it. Assuming the attack was acute and not chronic, you've got a long life ahead of you."

"What?"

"You're going to live."

And just like that, time started up again, and with it the usual sounds, smells, fears. Who was that fake angel of death, that pretty, painted clown who had delivered my fraudulent death sentence? I never saw her again, and when I told my doctor about her, he apologized profusely but had no clue who she was. They gave me new nurses, new nonslip socks, and a new room in intensive care. For the next week I fasted, received fluids through a drip, and got zonked on Dilaudid, but mostly I tried to figure out what the hell was wrong with me—which, in one way or another, was how I'd spent most of my life.

I only very peripherally remembered the pancreas from college biology. It is a six-inch slab of glandular meat located in the lower abdomen, and rediscovering it was like meeting a long-lost son—who'd come to kill me. The doctor told me I was lucky. "Pancreatitis attacks this severe often result in death." During an attack, amylase and lipase, the enzymes that the pancreas normally secretes to aid in digestion, rebel against their source; they try to sizzle the organ down through their chemical fire into an annihilated pile of self-digested slop. Primary causes: advanced alcoholism or gallstones. The CT scan convinced my doctors that I didn't have gallstones, and I convinced them that I wasn't an alcoholic.

So what had caused my pancreas to suddenly turn on itself?

I went on *zanka*—a leave of absence from the monastery—and flew to my parents' home in Wisconsin, where I promptly became both the star of, and audience for, a black comedy about the human body. My brother-in-law, a brilliant chiropractor and former triathlete, turned me on to a probiotic that boasted "Vaginally-derived beneficial bacteria from a healthy twenty-three-year-old woman." "The science is solid," he insisted. "I'm going to e-mail you a link. Order these vaginamins stat!"

I took them and reported the results: "Wicked gas." "I bet. It's like a fart and queef all at once," he e-mailed back.

I was on probiotics because I was on antibiotics: antibiotics to kill the bad bacteria, probiotics to foster good bacteria—which, my mother's nutritionist avowed, is essential for proper digestion. Of course the nutritionist was the one who had told me to get on the antibiotic in the first place. Per his orders I positioned a tiny plastic jar beneath my ass and strategically pinched a turd, which I then mailed to a company in Utah for analysis. They claimed I had parasites, a possible cause of pancreatitis—hence the antibiotics, the brutally strong Flagyl, on which I overdosed at one point, causing urine the color of stout beer and a brief hallucination involving a toadstool growing from my father's forehead.

Meanwhile, my mother had a hunch that the meat-free diet at the monastery had caused my pancreatitis. She served me pig and cow for every meal. Who was I to argue? I was eating vaginal bacteria derived from, I sometimes imagined, a healthy, attractive, and broke twenty-three-year-old comparative-religions grad student named Trinity or Star—so why not go in for a little meat therapy while I was at it?

Halfway through my convalescence I flew to LA to visit my mentor, the eccentric monk who introduced me to Zen practice and now lived in my old apartment in West Hollywood. I expected a spiritual pep talk, but instead he took a large black suitcase out of the closet. It looked like a doomsday device inside—levers, knobs, gauges, dials.

"Every cell in your body is like a battery, and the Powerful Multiwave Oscillator sends out electromagnetic Tesla waves that recharge them," he said, handing me the pamphlet that came with the device. A crudely sketched and topless woman, with bangs practically swimming out of her forehead like a fleet of exotic fish, held what appeared to be a cross between a magic wand and a horse penis.

My mentor exited the closet with the device, poured himself a glass of wine, and flipped a switch inside the black suitcase. A shimmering worm of electricity squiggled and sizzled inside the glass ball at the tip of the phallic wand. I touched it to my left side and closed my eyes: it was bright black inside my skull—blotches of color and bolts of feeling. I suppose this was because I was being charged like a battery.

"How do you feel?" he shouted.

"Foolish."

In fact I did feel something. Per the instruction manual, I'd stripped to my underwear. Now I was getting an erection. This was a little awkward. My mentor is gay, and we had certain boundaries in our relationship that I wanted to continue to observe.

"Give it a chance!" he said.

All signs indicated that my pancreatitis had been acute, a one-shot deal, and that I was now in recovery mode. But whatever caused the illness was still inside me. I could feel it. Or at least I thought I could. When you don't know why you got sick, just about anything can be the cure, and you never really know if you're finally getting better. You go round and round in circles, taking medicine that produces side effects that you imagine to be a new manifestation of the enigmatic illness, so you take another type of medicine, which produces more and different side effects, and what began as a simple pain in your side becomes a spiraling descent into the blackness at the core of your being. Exhaustion becomes depression, and depression becomes despair.

How much longer could I go on living like this? And was this really living? Again and again I asked myself, "What is wrong with you? Where did this sickness come from?" and again and again I came up short. I was terrified that the instant I stopped worrying about my illness it would return. I wanted to be sure that it was gone forever. But I would never be sure. The bad thing could happen to me again at any time, and there was nothing I could do about it. The next time around it might even kill me. The fact that I could not accept this was preventing me from getting on with my life.

"Tell me what you feel!" my mentor cried.

"I feel like my soul got so sick and out of balance that it actually caused the illness in my body," I shouted.

I flew back to Wisconsin and visited Holy Hill, a Catholic church near my parents' house. I prayed at the outdoor Stations of the Cross and met an old priest. He had plump hills of rolling muscle for an upper body, like a professional wrestler from the 1980s. I told him how I got busted for smoking pot in college and that I chose to pay for my crime by doing community service at Holy Hill.

"I'm glad we could be of service," he said.

I told him that I was a Zen monk on the verge of quitting the life.

"Oh," he exclaimed. "Oh ho ho!"

I asked him if he ever tired of the religious life.

"It is all tiresome," he said. "All of life."

I asked him what was the most interesting sin anyone ever confessed to him.

"Oh ho ho! I can't tell you that! I can tell you that people sin in very interesting ways."

"The Devil is dynamic," I said. "Do you actually believe in the Devil?"

"I lived in Las Vegas for thirty years before going to seminary. Thirty years! I've seen it all."

"Have you ever seen evil?"

His shirt must have been over a thousand years old. It was frayed and light black in the way of fabric that has lost its life on the back of a hardworking man. He turned from the life-sized crucified Christ, to me, half smiling, as though he'd had enough of this.

"You want to know when you've seen evil?"

I told him I did.

"When you've seen it in the mirror. Do you know what I'm talking about?"

"I do."

"And what do you do then?"

"Break the mirror?"

"You go down on your knees, and you go down fast and quick, that's what you do. There's no breaking any mirrors."

We walked the Stations of the Cross in reverse, which is a good way to do it, because Christ's condition improves with each stop. "Every man has his own demons. Your demon could be my angel, and the other way around, but every man has terrible demons, and the religious life *brings those demons out*."

I now had a name for my affliction.

"How do you fight demons?" I asked.

"You don't. You know what happens when you try? You wind up fighting the whole world around you, because everywhere you look you will see your own demons. That's the nature of this world."

"This is not a very reassuring conversation, Father."

"You have two choices with demons—either you fall under their spell or you fall under their sword. If you fall under their spell you wind up in hell. So you know what you have to do?"

"No."

"You have to let them slay you."

"How do I do that?"

"How should I know, they're your demons."

A few weeks later a nun from the monastery called to tell me that Kuru had wandered into the wilderness and never returned. "Probably coyotes," she said. It seemed like a terrible omen. That night I awoke with a shooting pain in my side. Or was it a shooting pain in my mind? I couldn't tell the difference anymore. I rolled out of bed, went downstairs and into the garage, opened the garage door, sat down on a folding chair, and collapsed into a full-blown spiritual crisis as rain pounded through the darkness before me.

I threw down with my demons until dawn. It was like my thoughts and emotions were attacking me just as the enzymes of my inflamed pancreas had attacked their source on a similar night three months ago. What was I doing in that garage? I was doing everything. I was arguing with myself, arguing with others in my head, praying, cursing, aching. What I remember most was wanting to sob, and just opening my mouth and—nothing coming out. That terrified me.

Then the dark night of the soul became whatever it becomes when the sun starts to rise, and I realized that I was too exhausted for any more of this shit. I had no more fight left in me. You cannot defeat your demons, for they thrive on the fight itself.

The lights went on inside the house. My mother the early bird was up preparing my all-beef breakfast. I really didn't want her to see me like this. She's one of my favorite people. I wasn't an easy birth, I wasn't an easy kid, and I didn't want to be a difficult adult on top of all that.

You have got to get it together. If not for yourself, then for Mom. So I got it together the only way I know how. I took a deep breath. Then I took another. I let the inhale and exhale do their thing. The mind has a mind of its own. It takes work to be simple and true, and when it's working, it's really no work at all.

Where do you go when your life is broken and the way back to yourself is lost? You go to your knees—or your butt, if you're a Zen monk. The moment I got sick a light went out, and since then I'd forgotten the most basic principle of Zen meditation: breathe into the place where you ache the most. For three months I'd obsessed over the pain in my gut, but not once had I inhabited this region through conscious breathing. I'd fallen deeper and deeper inside myself looking for the cause of my sickness, but the farther I went the more distance there was to go. I couldn't stop thinking—that was the *real* disease.

Breathing in the summer rain felt like throwing open the doors and windows on a house that had been boarded up for a century. Where was this breath coming from? Where did it go? It came and left me freely. Nature wanted to merge with itself, and I was the chosen means for this connection. All I had to do was breathe. So I did. I inhaled, and all of nature flowed through me. I exhaled, and all of nature flowed from me.

I was rooted to that chair for quite some time before an insight came upon me the way a deer appears in a silent forest: its presence, though heralded by a light pounding of the earth, somehow making the forest quieter still.

I am not really afraid of death.

Actually, I was a little bit pissed off at death. I'd faced it in the hospital, accepted it, and then it stood me up. Now I had to face an equally terrifying and profound prospect.

I have to go on living.

With that thought my mind stopped, and I heard the rain falling in the morning light through the open garage door. The true statement is the one that stops your mind and brings you back out of yourself into the world around you.

I felt something in my side again. It was not so much a sensation as a twitch of recognition, like the first kick of life in a mother's womb, the pulse that is equally self and other. It was the sound of the rain as the gut hears it, when the gut is listening. Water went from the sky into my belly, and then it was rolling down my cheeks and I could barely breathe because of my joy.

The experience—it was a moment of grace—took me back to the emergency room three months earlier, to the wails of the Mexican woman.

"Ay yiy yiy—give me something!"

When they wheeled her gurney past the open curtain I got a good look. Her hair, dyed red, was plastered against her engorged face. She threw back her head and opened her mouth and screamed. She looked like she wanted to kill every living thing in the building, especially her husband, a very large man who looked very small next to his larger-than-life wife.

Her legs were spread and her knees were pointed at the ceiling. Her belly was a galactic ball of fire. She was passing through the ER on her way to the maternity ward.

I want to say that our eyes met and that she saw that I was dying just as I saw that she was giving life; that the pain in her belly and the pain in mine were, like the inhale and the exhale, intimate partners in a single activity that was manifesting and dissolving the entire universe. I want to say that we both recognized that the birth in her and the death in me were two sides of the very same thing.

And what is this thing? I want to say, but I don't have the words, so I have to stop here, though we all know how this story ends. Every story ends with a death sentence, but the story doesn't end there.

However, if you want something more concrete, I went inside and ate my mother's all-meat meal. Then I returned to the monastery, picked out a new cat, and got serious about the practice of birth and death. This is Zen. It is the Great Matter. It is the whole spiritual project. And in truth, I hadn't even begun it yet. But if not now, when? A human being has a shelf life, and I was ripe.

8

How Deep Is Your Love?

The afternoon I was scheduled to meet the dying man, my laptop got stolen. The crime felt oddly intimate, as though a burglar had snuck into my bed one night and, without waking me, removed the underwear from my body—with his mouth. I cried a little in the parking lot of Ralph's grocery store, where the thief had broken into my Honda during the ten minutes that I was inside buying flowers. Fortunately, I had all my files backed up on a thumb drive. Unfortunately, I kept the thumb drive in the same bag as my Mac, so the thief got it too.

But wasn't that just like me? To leave the thumb drive in the same bag that I carry the computer around in? What the hell sense does that make?

It was at least a hundred degrees outside. The heat felt like a vice slowly crushing my skull from every direction. I'd recently said goodbye to cigarettes and was sucking down nicotine lozenges like candy and compulsively talking to myself. Over half of my next book, three years of a daily journal, a rough draft of a novel, one very terrible screenplay about a black rapper who goes into the Deep South in whiteface, dozens of completed or nearly completed essays and short stories—nearly half a million words. Gone. As I mentally prepared to visit the dying man, I felt like I was dying too. That laptop contained a portion of myself that I would never get back.

With such a key part of my identity now gone, I felt a compulsion to prove my existence. I couldn't just sit peacefully, like the Zen priest I am, while waiting to report the crime at the police station. I had to whip out my iPhone and check my e-mail. Then I checked Facebook. Then I checked my book ranking on Amazon. Then, because a sufficient amount of time had passed (ten seconds), I started over and checked my e-mail again, my thumbs banging the screen like a kid on a sugar high pounding a piano with two hammers.

How can a Zen priest be so self-absorbed and distractible? Perhaps meditation has simply honed my awareness to the point where I can clearly see how imperfect I am but has in no way helped me to change this fact. What a horrible practice! You know it's bad when you're blaming your meditation practice for the stress in your life. But I was heartbroken over all the work I'd lost and enraged at the universe for being chronically unfair, so I gave my better angels the finger and searched for affirmation on the Internet instead of powering down my phone, taking a deep breath, and accepting the fact that something dear to me was probably gone forever.

I met with a handsome young police officer who told me in so many words that my laptop was, for all practical purposes, on the missing person of Jimmy Hoffa, and that when they found *him*, I'd get my stolen words back. Then I set out for the medical center where, I imagined, the sick man was putting off dying until he could have a few words with me. The heat and the nicotine from the lozenges were giving me the kind of headache where your skull feels like the drum set in a Swedish death-metal band. My breath raced as I phoned the desk nurse from the clogged 10 Freeway.

"Please let the family know I'm running late."

There was a long silence. I'd called twice already to delay. "Hurry," she said. "He's not going to make it through the night."

"Sorry, sorry, I'm stuck in traffic," I said.

In reality, I was lost. I typed with my thumb while hitting the brakes and gas, and my iPhone told me where I needed to go. I need an app for spiritual guidance, I thought. I can't even let go of my laptop. How can I look into the dimming eyes of a dying man and tell him that he needs to let go of this life?

I searched the radio for inspiration. I was psyching myself up instead of calming down. Bad idea. Nobody wants to look up from their deathbed and see a priest smiling down at them like he just did a line of coke. I punched seek over and over and got The Bee Gees' "How Deep Is Your Love." Fantasy time: I imagined walking into a hospital room filled with Taiwanese people. Slow motion, my robes flowing behind me. I put my hand on the shoulder of the dying man's wife and simply erase her sadness with my smile. I hug the old grandmother. "You white but you okay!" she cries, and the whole family bursts into laughter. The dying man cracks a smile too. I take his hand and his eyes open. The wife's lower lip trembles. "He . . . he hasn't moved in seven days. But you . . . your presence . . . it moved him. Literally!"

Life went silent as I turned off the Honda in the medical center parking lot. Golfers swung silver clubs across the street; an orange grove sprawled for miles below me, speckles of fruit bedazzling the verdant valley. There were tears in my eyes thanks to the Bee Gees ballad, which was still buzzing through my nervous system like a gallon of coffee: "How deep is your love / how deep is your love / I really need to learn . . ."

I put my head on the steering wheel. I was in no way ready to face a dying man.

We once hosted a workshop at the monastery for recovering alcoholics. I befriended a philosophical nurse who rightly described herself as "beastly fat and very angry." I confessed to her that I hated being a monk. She confessed to me that she hated being alive. She went on: "Finally one day I realized—I am not obliged to try and enjoy this life of mine. I do not have to have a reason to go on living. I do not have to be a hero. All I have to do is suit up and show up."

Many are the moments when a layperson shows me how to be a monk. They nonchalantly offer these nuggets of diamond-tight, luminous wisdom as though they're telling me something that I already know, and I nod sagely as though I do, while thinking, "I'm going to use that."

Suit up and show up. I thought of this as my fingers threaded my priest's belt into a knot over my *koromo* robe. The hospital bathroom was like a green room where I was preparing for a performance, only I had no idea what my lines were. I studied myself in the mirror—thankfully, it assured me that I was a monk. But I stared a little too long, and for a split second I could have sworn that I glimpsed a frightened fraud beneath the frock.

Shirley, the large, angry nurse, had told me that she often had to force herself to play the role of compassionate caregiver. "Death is all around me in the hospital, but it always seems like the wrong people are dying. The assholes hang on to the bitter end," she explained. "People think that nurses just automatically give a damn, like it's in our genes. Let me tell you something—having the will to refrain from putting a pillow over the face of some bitter, dying bastard who also happens to be your patient is actually something you have to work at."

"It's just like being a monk," I said. "You fake it till you make it."

"No," she said, raising her eyebrow, a hairless slash of blue, "You fake it till you're not faking it anymore. It's called trying."

What a sight I must have made, stepping into the hospital room bald-headed in what appeared to be a long black dress with sleeves big enough to lift me off the ground with the right gust of wind. There were four Taiwanese people in the room, and three of them looked up at me. A quarter of the room was sick and dying, which is a large percentage and accounted for the leaden atmosphere. I knew that I was the headliner. What I didn't know was that there was an opening act, and she wanted my job. Tall and in her midfifties, her expression was permanent and hard to describe, as though she'd told a plastic surgeon, "Make me look like someone who has just heard a joke that she doesn't understand." Not surprisingly, she was gripping a Bible.

Her considerably shorter husband stood behind her, glaring at me as though he hoped I might use my Buddhist black magic to simply vanish off the face of the earth in a puff of sulfurous smoke. He was holding his wife's hand, and she was holding the hand of an alert, shockingly young woman with the flushed pink face of a mother in labor, who was in turn holding her sick husband's unresponsive hand. He was a blur on the bed in the corner of my eye. I could not quite look at him yet, for his wife seemed to want something from me. She could not reach out and shake my hand, weighed down as she was by Christianity on the one side and Death on the other. Like me, she seemed to be playing a role—the role of hostess at her husband's deathbed.

When the tall woman saw my robes and my big bald head, her eyes went wide and she started gabbling furiously. Everyone's eyes closed, then opened, and there was some post-prayer conversation, full of tired smiles, hugs, and goodbyes. I understood nothing of what they said, but all deathbed conversation is the same. Really straightforward, often mundane things—hospital food or plans for the evening—are discussed with a whispering intensity reserved for the Situation Room. People are exhausted and completely vitalized at the same time. Nothing like death to bring a little life to the room.

Then it was just me, the wife, and the dying man. "Sorry about that. We *were* Christian. Five years ago we converted to Buddhism," she said, rolling her eyes. I nodded. If there's anything that intense Christians are useful for, it's helping non-Christian strangers bond.

I took a wooden mallet and a *mokugyo* drum the size of a grapefruit out of my backpack. I passed the wife a chant book. The desk nurse had told me that the wife requested two things, a prayer and a blessing for her husband. "Zen monks don't really do either of those things," I tried to explain. Chanting was my substitute for a prayer. I didn't know yet what my substitute for a blessing would be.

I watched the wife sink into her uncomfortable chair in a kind of dead-relaxed stupor. Then she began weeping. I wanted to get up out of my own uncomfortable chair and hug her, but I felt weird about doing this in front of her ailing husband, as though he might suspect that I was trying to poach her right before his dying eyes. And who knows, maybe the thought crossed my mind. During times of sublime anguish, I sometimes can't distinguish intense feelings of love from sexual urges.

I still have an image in my head of this young woman sitting up impeccably straight, her hands folded in her lap over her fashionable black pants, shedding, it seemed to me, the perfect number of tears, right down to the very last one. They streamed down her face and throat and turned the white collar of her blouse gray.

She chanted like a champ and we made our way through the Heart Sutra, the Dharani of Compassion, and the ten-page, sleep-inducing excerpt from the Lotus Sutra. We both faced her husband, but I still hadn't really looked at him yet. After I brought the chanting home with a warbling flourish, the wife stood up. We were on either side of the dying man. Her cheeks and eyes were glistening and she seemed refreshed, like the sky after a good, quick rain.

"I will introduce you to my husband."

For the first time I really took him in, and I felt the truth of the phrase *My heart goes out to you*. He had the face of a child. His young body was twisted, his spine arched, so that it looked like he was gouging into the bed with his shoulder blades. It was as though you'd swung a baseball bat into his back a week ago, and he was still frozen in that initial contortion of pain. His eyes were wide open. There was nothing drugged about them. Everything else about him looked drugged, but not those eyes.

I once cornered a wood rat in a bathroom. As I bent over with a bucket to try and capture it with the intention of then throwing it into the toilet and flushing it into oblivion, I looked into its eyes. They looked back. The body of this little animal was quivering, its tiny shoulders shaking in fast forward, and in its eyes I saw the pure sentient terror of a creature the instant before its life is snatched away.

I saw that same animal terror in this man's eyes.

I had come to the blessing part of his wife's request. I needed to do something. I took his hand out from under the blanket. It was limp and lukewarm; life was leaving it. I said his name and put my hand on his chest. I kept looking in his eyes, but I couldn't find purchase there. There was no bottom to his suffering.

His wife was weeping openly now. There was something happening here, and I finally realized what it was. I was giving him his last rites. No one would come after me. There was no other priest waiting in the wings. I was the one they had contacted.

Me. The guy who still had "How Deep Is Your Love" running through his head.

Fake it till you're not faking it anymore.

So I held his hand, lowered my head, mentally collapsed every last bit of distance between us—as best I could, anyway—and I wished his butchered and bleeding soul well. You better believe I said a prayer. I sent it out into the universe through our two bodies. And yes I wanted it to be over, because I was ashamed that I might be doing it wrong and embarrassed that his wife was watching me and possibly judging my sincerity. But I held his hand tightly, for the both of us. I looked in this dying man's eyes and I saw myself.

We somehow became equals. I found a point of connection, and I held him there.

I closed my eyes, and when I opened them I felt my whole face reborn as just this crumpled, ruined mask. I could hide nothing. I wasn't sure if it was appropriate that I was crying a little, but it's not like I could help it. Something had happened in that desperate and intimate moment. We both held hands and let go together.

The wife seemed happy and totally done with me, but in a good way. We made some small talk about reincarnation in the hallway outside the room. Then she slipped me a small golden envelope, which I opened in the parking lot as the sun set behind the marvelous orange orchard below me. There was a hundred dollar bill inside, which I used to buy a very large, meat-based dinner, chased by a pair of nicotine lozenges.

As I drove home, I remembered Dr. Haley, a dear friend of Roshi's, who'd died six months earlier. The funeral home was in the middle of the desert I was now driving through; it was a brand-new building in a scorching, windswept valley, like real estate from planet Mars.

The sufficiently sepulchral mortician at the front desk had pointed us to a dark corridor that led to a side room with a faint glow. I figured that we were supposed to wait there until they took us in the back to visit the body, at which point I planned to excuse myself for the bathroom and then repair to a non-windy corner of the building outside for a much-needed cigarette. But when I pushed my teacher and his wheelchair around the corner and into the small, bare room, there was—to my utter shock—a dead body in a big black box. It was Dr. Haley–like, but it was not him at all. The candlelit creature inside the casket was a thing unto itself, the embodiment of the natural phenomenon known as death.

In real life, Dr. Haley had towered. In real death, he seemed about three feet shorter. This is what happens when you drain the fluids from a body, I thought. We're 60 percent water, after all. His stiff white hair was spazzing out at odd angles, like the plastic hair of an old doll that hasn't been played with for decades. The back of his skull was propped up by a steel post instead of a pillow. Everything about him looked awkward—he was a Dr. Haley impostor—everything, that is, except for his face.

I wheeled Roshi right up to the very edge of this silent spectacle, just as I'd done when we visited the Grand Canyon. Lizzie removed a tiny mokugyo from her tote bag and lit a stick of incense. We chanted the Heart Sutra. It was as though we were singing a song of reverence before some miracle of nature, a streaking comet or an animal giving birth. Unlike every other human face I've ever looked into, there was absolutely nothing wrong with this one. Living human faces register nearly endless variations on the theme of suffering, but Dr. Haley's face stayed the same from instant to instant.

It was absolutely silent, and so was I.

As though to confirm everything I was feeling, Lizzie turned to me and said, "He looks so peaceful."

I said, "He's done running," and she seemed to know what I meant.

The mountain was dark and silent when I returned to the monastery after my visit with the dying man. A veil of mist inked the footpaths black. I sat down on the only rock where I get wireless access, popped a lozenge, took out my iPhone, and fed my addiction to nicotine and attention. Looking into that screen, waiting for the pages to load, waiting for *something*, was like looking into the dying man's eyes—there was nothing to grab on to. It was bright and bottomless.

I looked up into the vast night sky, so dark, silent, and sure of itself. Nothing new about it in all the years I've known it, yet it only gets more interesting. Later, tossing and turning in bed, I was still compulsively searching, this time inside my own skull, searching for something that wasn't fleeting, that wouldn't perish, that I could hold on to forever, even in deep sleep.

But you cannot Google your own soul.

Hmm, I thought, that's good. I should tweet that. Right now, before I forget!

Why? Because I had something genuine to share or simply because I wanted to be heard? Did I tweet, and write, as an offering to others or to shore up my feelings of permanence and relevance against a cosmos that is like a great thief who takes everything in the end, all our words and deeds? The loss of my laptop was just the beginning, and minor in comparison to what the dying man and his wife were losing, and which we will all lose sooner or later.

Yet I couldn't stop thinking about it. I tried to picture the face of the guy who filched my MacBook Air, and my stomach turned and my mind puked a little. Maybe it was a woman, a bony-fingered meth addict. She had all my words. What was she doing with them? Perhaps the real truth was that I did not fear death so much as I feared leaving this planet without leaving my mark on it in some way, dying without accomplishing anything, as though I'd never existed at all. And now this toothless crystal fiend was out there somewhere erasing my legacy!

But if something can be taken from you, was it ever truly yours to begin with? It occurred to me that the harder we search for something permanent in this world, the more ephemeral and disposable are the things we find, and the more we find ourselves simply searching for the sake of searching, moving for the sake of moving.

We are a culture running away from death.

Maybe, in the end, death is the only thing that cannot be taken from us; maybe it's the only thing we can truly call our own. When I held that dying man's hand, closed my eyes, and disappeared into the diminishing warmth of his palm, I felt for a brief instant like we were owning our imminent deaths together, and that he was blessing me as much as I was blessing him. It was nothing like my Bee Gees–fueled fantasy, where I held his hand and his eyes popped open, full of life. Instead, we held hands and died a little together, and so came to resemble Dr. Haley, who was done searching. Maybe that's why his face was so peaceful, a peace every bit as deep as the suffering in the dying man's eyes.

How deep is your love, how deep is your love—that song was still trapped in my head, only now my inner Barry Gibb seemed to be asking for an answer. Not so deep, I told him. I crave immortality, I'm attached to things and ideas like my stolen laptop and those lost words, and I really need a smoke. But I'll keep faking it until I'm not faking it anymore, I thought, drifting into a bottomless sleep from which I would awaken tomorrow, but the dying man would not.

I'll keep trying.

9

The Surrender Bender

In my first memory of Daishin, he is on his knees, tucking the top *kimono* part of my disheveled student robes into the bottom *hakama* part. He looks up at me from under vintage wire-rim glasses. His warm blue eyes are a good place for your own eyes to land when you're anxiously glancing to and fro.

It is my first weeklong *dai-sesshin* retreat. I've been minding my own mind on the cushion for five days, but now I have a job. He has just given me detailed instructions on how to serve a Zen meal—a formal affair with bells and clappers and chanting that is only slightly less choreographed than a Broadway musical. He is fit, vibrant, sixty going on thirty, and speaks with a trace of a lisp, like an extremely intelligent child.

"Zen practice is strict, but the great thing about it is that even if your life is falling apart and you're a total mess inside, at least your robes are on straight." He rolls his shoulders back. He does this a lot. Such gestures are both rhythmic and compulsive, like he's taught his tics to dance. "A formal meal isn't a performance.

It's a practice. Zen is a practice that you teach yourself." He hands me the bronze gong to ring the zendo down for breakfast. "If you get lost during the meal, I'll be right here." He points to the table at the far end of the dining hall.

I am looking at that table now. It's a decade later. The dining hall is empty. Daishin is speaking to me through the phone. He's just given me the diagnosis. If it were up to me, cancer would target assholes, and the cure would be: stop being an asshole. But cancer does not have human logic. It does not have a human heart. Six months later I rent a thirty-foot RV and set out for Daishin's deathbed with Roshi and Lizzie. The trip is complicated by the fact that Roshi is dying too, slowly, of old age. He is like the sun, setting. Still luminous, but there's less and less of him on our side. The trip is his idea, but can he make it?

Not long ago, cancer came for Lucy, our temple cat—ate her from the inside out. The vet put her down one morning, which seemed like a strange time to die, as everyone was going to work, and the sun was shining, and the birds were chirping and landing on the windowsill.

I've lost pets, friends, family, and more than a few illusions this past year. Some days, I feel haunted by the ghosts of grief, which take the form of anger, resentment, despair—the howling banshees of the inner life. We so desperately want to find something to hold on to, but everything changes, everything dies, and so we grasp after absences, we hurl our hearts into the vacuum where the things that we have loved and lost used to be. One thing I've learned is that grief only ends when we can let go of the idea that there is something outside of us that can make us whole, and that that something is now gone.

"Oh nuts!" Lizzie shouts.

I pull the RV off the 10 Freeway into the parking lot of a community college. It is empty but lit like a football stadium. This is helpful, for I am looking into Roshi's stomach through a dark slit where his rubber feeding tube has popped out.

"You were too rough when we moved him from his chairlift to the RV," Lizzie says. Nearly six feet tall, sinewy, her face lightly pocked ("That's my termite damage," she said as I touched her face years ago when we were lovers), Lizzie moves quickly and clearly through life, and expects the same from others. Her eyes are steady and bright this evening, but her spiky brown hair cannot decide which direction it wants to go in.

After Roshi's brutal struggle with aspiration pneumonia, the doctors told us that he would be dead within a week. The G-tube was supposed to be a temporary measure to give him nutrition before his imminent passing. That was two and a half years ago. The G-tube is now gnarled and flesh-brown from multiple feedings, extending from a hole in his side like a rubber umbilical cord. Roshi is a fighter. He is making death take its time.

We do a U-turn, drive back to LA, and park in the street outside our temple. It's midnight. Lizzie retrieves a new G-tube from Roshi's apartment and, with the steady hands of a Civil War surgeon on the battlefield, pops it into his stomach with a fleshy slurp. My job is to look on and nearly faint.

We sleep in the RV. A flock of wild parrots wakes us at dawn. We tell Roshi that the trip is over. We are worried that it will kill him.

"Don't give up," he says.

"Arizona is hot, okay? And it's far away. If the heat doesn't kill him he's going to keel over and die from exhaustion," I tell Lizzie.

She studies Roshi, who is lying motionlessly on the couch. His full-time caregiver for five years, she is the "Roshi whisperer," and one very good reason that he has lived to be 107 years old.

"He wants to go," she says.

I knew she was going to say that.

We complete the seven-hour drive by 6:00 p.m. and arrive on Daishin's doorstep wired and smelling of cold-pressed coffee. Faith, Daishin's wife, reaches up and hugs me with her thin arms.

A small crowd is gathered in the living room of this tightly appointed adobe home. Daishin sits on the couch, wearing a hakama skirt and a linen shirt. His legs are up on a table. None of his pants fit anymore. His calves are as bulbous as Popeye's forearms. His collarbone protrudes nakedly, like rebar. He looks like a skeleton from the waist up and a sumo wrestler from the waist down. My eyes travel up the sharp lines of his ravaged upper body. The higher I go the worse it gets, until I arrive at his face. There is more death in it than Daishin.

I hug him—his hard skeleton. I am smiling like someone who's been punched in the gut. I despise myself for not knowing what to say. He doesn't stop me when I put my hand on his swollen thigh. I stroke a small, safe patch of it that I've staked out as my area of responsibility. I stroke and stroke and I'm crying in my throat.

There is a lot of hullaballoo around Roshi, who is nearly unconscious with fatigue. Several of Daishin's students are creating a makeshift bed for him out of tables, cushions, a spare mattress.

"We're here for one reason—because Roshi said 'Don't give up,'" Lizzie, Roshi's PR person, announces.

"See," shouts a young, bald man, fluffing a pillow. "Don't give up!"

The student is referring to a last ditch lifesaving treatment that is being whispered about. However, deep within Daishin's warm blue eyes there is clarity and understanding. He gives me those eyes for a second. We always had an unspoken understanding, two soft and anxious men trying to teach ourselves Zen—the art of knowing when to hold tight and when to let go. I can read his mind: *I am not fighting for my life anymore. I am struggling to let go of it.*

Roshi sleeps for twenty-four hours straight. We are trying to keep him alive; we are trying to help Daishin die. It is a little confusing. At one point we put the two of them in bed together. The sun is rising in that merciless way that it has after you've been up all night. Daishin's cat curls up between them. "Is this a Kodak moment?" Faith asks.

Later, I sit down before a bowl of oatmeal. Daishin breathes heavily on the couch in the corner of my eye. I try to eat invisibly. My fear is that he wants me to go back to LA, but he's too kind to ask. People's character traits are amplified on their deathbed, and Daishin's instinct is to give. The last thing I want to do is prevail upon him with my presence when he needs all his energy just to breathe.

He whispers. I rush to his side. Oxygen hisses from a cannula into his nostrils. His eyes keep rolling around in his head. His voice trails off into non sequiturs.

"I can't talk," he finally rasps.

"That's a first," I say.

He smiles with his eyes closed. "Let's watch TV."

And this is where the afternoon gets weird. First of all, he is flipping through the stations when a commercial comes on from an ambulance-chasing law firm: "If you have mesothelioma, join us in a class-action law suit!" It's kind of a moment, because mesothelioma is the cancer that Daishin is dying from.

Yes! I think. *Let's sue somebody!*

"Ugh," he says, and changes the channel.

He stops on the David Lynch art-house film *The Elephant Man*. It is so depressing that it makes me feel as though I am also dying of cancer. Daishin is transfixed. Gradually the movie takes hold of me. Every half hour I help Daishin walk across the stone floor and back, for a little exercise, but our eyes never leave the TV.

The film is based on the life of Joseph Merrick, a saintly but deformed Victorian-era Englishman played with sweet sophistication by John Hurt. As I massage Daishin's swollen feet I can't help but notice that he, like the Elephant Man, is trapped in a monstrous body. I am in a heightened state of viewing. Every image enters me like a divine vision. When you're dying, or with the dying, you need art, not bullshit. Real art is not about how hopeless things are, it's about what human beings do in the face of all that hopelessness.

I have seen this movie before. In college I even acted in *The El-ephant Man* stage play—furthermore, I was in the final, climactic scene. Yet my mind refuses to remember how this damn story ends.

Over the Elephant Man's hospital bed there hangs a picture of a child sleeping softly. If the Elephant Man lies down like the boy in that picture he will suffocate to death due to his massively deformed skull. Yet, fully lying down is his dream. It signals the peace and normalcy that have always eluded him. After a particularly spectacular evening that includes his receiving a standing ovation at the London opera, the Elephant Man stands alone in his hospital room and gazes at the picture of the sleeping child. Then he studies a photo of his beloved deceased mother at his bedside.

Then he lies down fully in his bed.

And here the film dissolves into a surreal Lynchian sequence. Stars float past us. The haunting violins of Samuel Barber's *Adagio for Strings* build. The disembodied voice of the Elephant Man's mother whispers over the appearance of her spectral image in the cosmic backdrop.

"Never never, nothing will die.

"The stream flows, the wind blows . . . the heart beats . . ."

An eclipsed sun appears, along with dark clouds, which are sucked backward into the mother's image.

"Nothing will die."

Fade out.

That night I lay awake on a bed of *zabutan* cushions in the zendo behind the house. The final words of the movie play on an endless loop in my head as images of Daishin's and the Elephant Man's swollen limbs merge and become indistinguishable.

Nothing will die.

Is it true? I try to picture my own death. I wonder if I should donate to a sperm bank to keep my bloodline going. It is an appealing thought, turning my most embarrassing habit into my most enduring legacy. Try as I might, though, I cannot sustain any coherent thought regarding my own inevitable ultimate absence. It is one of life's ironies that the greatest truth about the human condition is also the hardest to imagine.

"I don't know why this is happening to me," Daishin told me that afternoon. "I'm just really sad I won't be able to practice with you anymore. When I'm gone, that also means you'll be gone to me."

That's when I lost it.

"It's okay," he said, patting my hand, "I'm tired of struggling with my demons."

The first time we roomed together at the monastery, he said, "Sometimes you may find me a little difficult to work with. I have some problems." Then he dumped out his entire suitcase, spread his tube socks and toiletries and *Vanity Fair* magazines across the floor, and spent the next hour rearranging them on the carpet according to some private pattern that only he understood. Later that night, he showed no sign of embarrassment when I caught him alone in the washroom, talking to the mirror.

"Sometimes I talk to myself," he said. Then he went back to flossing his teeth.

It was one of the many moments where I fell in love with him all over again. Daishin never pretended that he had his shit together. He taught me that you cannot be something other than yourself, no matter how enlightened you pretend to be, and so you must manifest yourself fully, each and every moment; you must bring all your subterranean selves, all your thoughts and feelings, no matter how grim and unbearable, to the surface, and to completion—dissolving them through your connection to the world around you so that a new pure self, and a new world along with it, can arise the next instant.

Now, on his deathbed, Daishin is bringing his life, his very self itself, to completion. I cannot emphasize enough just how exhausting it is trying to help him die. The job gets harder and harder the closer he gets. You want to save him, but this is not about what you want. You have to help him let go, which means you have to let go too, over and over.

We are on a surrender bender.

The zendo door swings open at 6:00 a.m. I make out Faith's outline in the rising sun. "He told me to call hospice. They'll be here by two this afternoon."

Death moves quickly, through the shadows, like a predator in the night. It is there, then it is not . . . then suddenly you're staring in its eyes. Within the hour Daishin is palpably weaker. Faith, so thin, so light, cannot lift him by herself anymore. Suddenly I am essential to this operation. And what an operation it is. Daishin has turned the seemingly straightforward act of dying into one of his usual complicated procedures, with his special rules and rituals and slightly nonsensical ways of doing things.

He's doing this thing where he says "One . . . two . . . three!" at which point Faith and I are supposed to pull him to his feet so that he can—what? Get some exercise? On his deathbed? The problem is, he counts off "One . . . two . . . three . . ." and then he does not move. Instead he keeps on counting: "four . . . five . . . six . . ." and then suddenly tries to get up at a random number of his choosing.

"Tailbone," he says, when he finally stands.

Of his many pains, the one just above his butt is the worst. He is emaciated and his tailbone is jutting out like a large marble—sitting on it is torture. The cure for this is apparently a spanking.

"Go ahead," he says.

I sort of shiatsu the aching protrusion.

"Ahhhhh," he says, shaking his tail feathers.

"Every room he walks into automatically becomes a better place," I tell Faith. She laughs: "I think so. But he drives some people crazy!"

Now it's time for his hourly constitutional. He has this all worked out. Faith stands in front of him, facing forward. He puts his hands on her shoulders. I stand behind him. "Brace me," he says. I put my hands on his hip bones. He lifts one twenty-pound foot. Puts it down. Lifts the other. Puts it down. We are like a very slow-moving conga line.

It takes us ten minutes to walk a few feet and back. He collapses on the couch and puts his lips to a water bottle but does not suck. I realize that he is, through repetition and ritual, turning his death into a spiritual exercise, albeit a torturous one.

"Do you want a spike?" Faith asks.

"I'll have a spike," he gasps.

Faith hands him a painkiller and makes a mark in a notebook. I sit down and close my eyes beside him on the couch. I keep having these random memories. This time I'm facing him on the stone steps outside the monastery office. I'm so angry I can almost taste it in my mouth. I scream at him because I do not know what else to do and because he will take it—I blame his whole generation of *oshos*, or Zen priests, for the problems we are facing in our community, problems that have nothing to do with him, and he nods and never flinches or breaks eye contact, and later, when I return to my cabin, I discover that he has gone down the hill during his hour break and bought me a coffee and an oatmeal scone and put it on my desk, and when I see him again he apologizes because he knows I probably wanted a blueberry muffin instead.

"Scones are my thing, I know you have more of a sweet tooth. I can go back down ..."

I want to thank him now for that scone. *You're not the only one with demons*, I want to say. *Thank you for helping me exorcize mine.*

Lizzie shouts from the bedroom: "Coming!"

She wheels Roshi into the living room. He's lost too much weight this past year. He looks like a miniature version of himself, his features distinct but diminished, like the branches of a bonsai tree. He has become a highly specialized human being; he's almost not there, and yet he's completely present. Lizzie rolls his wheelchair next to the couch. His eyes are shut and he's slumped forward. The trip has nearly killed him.

"Ohayo Gozaimasu!" I shout in his good ear. "Good morning Roshi!"

He opens his mouth and shuts it.

I whisper, "We have to be careful when hospice comes or they might walk off with the wrong guy."

Lizzie cuts me in two with one glance.

Fuck, that was inappropriate. Fuck I'm tired. Being mean is a defense mechanism, my way of swimming away from the escalating undertow of Death in this house.

Roshi and Daishin are separated by Daishin's bare feet, which are propped up on a footstool between the two of them. Roshi's eyes pop open and these feet are the first thing he sees—inches from his face, as enormous as a pair of astronaut's boots. In Japanese culture it is a great insult to show the master the bottoms of your feet. Roshi studies them with that new expression of his (every time he nearly dies, as he nearly did two-and-a-half years ago, he comes back with a new expression), which is like a baby lying in a crib, staring up at a glittering mobile.

Daishin points to his feet: "Not so delicate."

Roshi nods. His eyes remain alert and alive and they are the focus of the room. He reaches out and takes each of Daishin's feet in his hands. I don't know why he does this, but it is perfect. They stay like this, connected through Daishin's feet, for ten minutes, then twenty, and then for I don't know how long. Daishin is in a kind of connection coma. Roshi's eyes are shut and his chin is tilted down. The flesh of his face sags, as though it might slip right off his skull. It's all they can do to sit before the big picture window, with the sun shining off their bald heads, and say goodbye.

Daishin is gazing at Roshi. The harder death crushes down on him, the shinier his eyes become, like two coal pieces being pressed into diamonds.

"What a teacher," he says.

The image of him gazing at our teacher will stay with me until my own death. But it is not my last memory of Daishin. This comes next, and it dovetails perfectly with my first memory of him.

I am filling my water bottle in the kitchen when I hear a loud banging on the front door. I rush into the living room and see a transport van in the driveway through the window. Faith opens the front door. Two goofy grim reapers from hospice walk in. Biff and Sparky are loud and their shirts are too small for their barrel chests. They don't take off their shoes. They act as though they're here to pick up a broken refrigerator. Faith takes a clipboard and signs some papers. It's all happening so fast. Biff and Sparky position the clattering hospice gurney beside the couch and lunge for Daishin.

"Hold on!" I shout, "Come on now."

Faith and Lizzie and I help Daishin to his feet. We sit him down on the gurney. I go on my knees before him, as he once went on his knees before me, to fix my robes, and with what I hope is the same gentleness I lift his legs and pivot his torso and lay him across the gurney. Maybe there is some possessiveness in my gesture. People behave strangely around the dying. They want to be the ones who matter.

Roshi is sitting in his chair across the room. He is made out of electricity. Daishin is distilled down to his very essence, pure consciousness with just enough juice left over to keep his heart pumping. They are locked onto each other. Biff and Sparky go on either side of Daishin and take the gurney handles and begin to wheel him toward the door. Daishin folds his hands in the *gassho* prayer mudra, his eyes staying on our teacher, and then fanning out across the room, touching all of us.

Lizzie bursts into tears. She begins wailing, almost screaming. Daishin tilts his head a little to one side, as though he doesn't quite understand.

"You can come see me in the hospital. Okay?"

And this is my final memory of Daishin: his hands in gassho as he is wheeled backward through the front door. Those warm blue eyes never leaving us.

He dies two days later.

A memorial service is scheduled at our LA temple. I few days beforehand, I ask Faith to give a eulogy. I ask an old Zen priest. I ask one of Daishin's friends. They all decline: if they have to get up there and talk about him, they will start crying. And so the task falls to me.

I'm pretty sure I won't cry. There is a part of me that wants to throw this life away simply because I do not understand death and all that comes with it—the pain, futility, sadness. It is a constant struggle, especially as I grow older and death grows nearer; it gets harder and harder to find reasons to go on living. I want to give up. I want to stop trying. I want to take a nap—for three hundred years. But every time I close my eyes, I see Daishin.

Once, I shouted at him from my bunk bed that the only way I was getting up that morning was to go to the medicine cabinet and swallow a whole bottle of aspirin. He laughed at me from under his glasses and rolled his shoulders back.

"Just maintain."

On those difficult days, when he could not operate at full capacity as a human being, rather than give up and backslide into depression or sloth, Daishin would tell himself, "Just maintain," over and over. "Don't give up, just maintain."

He taught me the difference between giving up and letting go, between despair and surrender. I have to let go of the anger I feel about Daishin's death, but I cannot give up on the whole human condition, cannot write it off as an ugly and stupid little experiment enacted by a cruel and indifferent universe. I must give death its due. Here's the key to grieving properly: you must completely die with the deceased and be reborn without him. If you can't do this, you will be haunted forever by the ghosts of grief.

We the living tend to privilege the values of life: strength, courage, youth, victory, expansion. But these values don't occur in a vacuum. Death is an equal if opposite activity, working in tandem with life. It is the vessel through which life flows, the space into which it grows—until the growing is over. Then the tables are turned and life upholds and nurtures death, until death is complete, giving way to the birth of something new. Death has its own values, which are often alien and frightful to the living: weakness, closure, darkness, surrender, contraction. Zen practice is about learning to accept the activity of death in the midst of life, so that ultimately we can manifest the values of both life and death with total freedom.

Daishin knew this. He told me, "I'm ready for death." But death comes when it is ready, not when you are ready. What I saw during Daishin's last days was a monk struggling to welcome his own demise. True surrender means that you let something happen to you on its terms, not your own.

The night before the memorial service I sit in the zendo at our LA temple, where Daishin practiced the art of dying and being reborn on the cushion for so many years. I realize that in his final days he gifted me with a vision of the ultimate practice: total surrender to the dying activity. Such is the crux of the eulogy I carefully craft and memorize.

Before he died, Faith told Daishin, "I'll miss you," and he said, "You'll feel me in the spaces between things." The morning of his memorial service it is as though he is speaking to me from the spaces between things. Mourners arrive and I feel none of their sorrow. When the time comes, I stand before eighty people at the head of our zendo. I close my eyes, as I always do when I speak before crowds.

And then I can't speak.

I have this image in my head—Daishin sitting beside me on the couch as we watch *Elephant Man* together.

Never, never, nothing will die.

The stream flows, the wind blows . . . the heart beats. . . .

I stand up there for a whole minute without saying anything.

It does not feel right to try and hold my shit together at Daishin's funeral, and so I let go. For a good three minutes. These are not loud sobs, just obvious ones, and they won't stop. I bite my lip until I can taste blood, but this only works if you're trying not to laugh. Nothing works if you're trying not to cry.

Finally the words come. And I tell everyone the story I just told you.

PART TWO

The Four Deaths
of My Teacher

10

Two and Three

1. The End of an Era; or, Fetish Aprons No More!

Once upon a time, in the prelapsarian days before the scandal, the monastery was gifted with a dozen shiny black faux-leather kitchen aprons. Not so unusual. Nonprofits are the recipients of many failed experiments in capitalism. Sometimes (like when we got twenty bags of cappuccino-flavored potato chips) it feels like businesses are just out there asking themselves, Was it a really bad idea? Did it not work and do we have seven hundred boxes of it in storage? Let's give it to the monks!

One morning, I was alone in the kitchen with Hank, the *tenzo*, or cook. Hank is husky, hairy, and horny—full of life—whereas I am frightened of life, people, and myself. He has a deep rich belly laugh, and one of the surest ways to mitigate my unremitting anxiety is to get him going so that I can hear it. He grabbed a pair of vegetable scrap buckets and left for the compost pits. "See you in a bit," I said. Then I peeled off my jacket, sweatshirts, boots, jeans, long underwear, and boxer briefs. I slid one of those black pleather aprons over my naked body, sat on a chair, and crossed my "little bitch gams," in Hank's parlance.

Moments later he came barreling through the door. I slapped the table with my belt and roared in a German accent, "Hallo chubby boy! Velcome to my keetchen!"

This came to be known as the Fetish Apron Incident.

That was, what, five years ago? It feels like 1962. I bring this up for one reason: Those days are over. You cannot, following a deep, painful sexual scandal, ever again carelessly perch your naked balls on a wooden chair in the kitchen and make sadomasochistic overtures to a peer.

Do you see what we have lost?

For years and years everybody slept with everybody at American Zen centers. So I am told. By the people who did the sleeping around. Who are now of the advanced age where non-embarrassing sexual intercourse is a fond memory that they like to continually invoke in your presence. My generation showed up to practice right in time for the sex scandals that one after another rocked the American Buddhist scene. Now if you sleep with one of your students you need a presidential pardon. Fucking hippies. Who, by the way, will get the last laugh. This very moment they're making sweet love without condoms in luxurious nursing homes as their bloated generation drains Social Security, so that by the time we're their age we'll be living alone under a bridge with a tinfoil hat and dumpster-diver breath. No geriatric intercourse for us!

Such are my thoughts, anyway, while waiting in the Southwest terminal at LAX. I'm about to board a plane for Wisconsin. Thanksgiving is three days away. I'm getting out of Dodge. It's been a little under a week since the scandal broke. I have successfully avoided the *New York Times* and *Los Angeles Times*, as well as a number of other media outlets, but our community is in a growing state of crisis over how to respond to the online allegations about . . . Roshi's sexualized teachings? Sexual misconduct? Sexual assault? We don't even know how to talk about this. There are so many different views—it is like *Rashomon* set in a SoCal monastery. For every woman who posts a detailed account of Roshi's sexual misconduct, another woman phones the office and tells me how Roshi used sexual touch the way ancient Zen masters used blows from their sticks—as a means to wake confused people up.

I am heartsick. I am also angry. I'm angry at the flaming fuckwits in our community who are still in denial. "Did Roshi really touch all those women? Or . . . ?" Or what, you moron? You think every one of them is lying? Because it's really fun to publicly accuse your former teacher of grabbing your vagina? I'm furious at the hypocrite monks who studied with Roshi for decades, knew what was going on all along, and are now publicly denouncing him, and, worst of all, full-on scapegoating those of us currently living at the monastery, as though they weren't covering up his behavior back when the old bastard was in his prime. I'm enraged at the Zen teachers outside of our community who are lining up, one after another, to kick us in the face, spurting platitudinous think pieces all over the Internet as though they alone, each one of them, has discovered for the very first time that "there are serious power differentials between a teacher and a student," ergo "sexual congregation between said parties is unacceptable." (They are, almost to a person, men, a group of people I am coming to hate.) And you know, I'm angry with my whole damn community, all of us, because those generic "morality porn" takedowns, every last wretchedly written one of them, are basically right. You don't finger-bang your student. End of story.

Please forgive me. I have to get this out. And it comes out violently. It triggers me. I trigger you. Consider this a trigger warning.

I'm angry with Roshi. I want to spit in his face.

But weirdly, I have no violence in me toward him. I would never spit in his face. I just, I shake my head and then these tears start coming, coming out of a face frozen in this rictus of a question that I can't figure out how to form.

And oh, I'm angry with myself, and that anger is turning to self-hatred, a total perversion of the Buddhist teaching of *anatta*, or not self. I am the polar opposite of all Zen monk clichés. My brain waves are not parked in equanimous alpha. When I chant, butterflies do not exit my gas hole.

It all began nine months ago, when Roshi suffered through a near-fatal bout of aspiration pneumonia. Right up to the day he got sick he was actively teaching. Now he will never again meet with a Zen student except for tea and minimal conversation. So many of us lost our teacher that day. This was Roshi's first death, the death of his role as our spiritual guide.

Then, a few days ago, an ex-monk published an exposé on a Zen website detailing Roshi's long history of sexual behavior with female students. The Buddhist Internet is going apeshit. Major media outlets are picking it up. The story is going viral and I'm witnessing Roshi's second death, the death of his public reputation—his name.

My father is waiting for me at the Milwaukee airport. "Hey Magoo. How was your flight?"

"Good. I sat next to this crazy guy who was talking to himself the whole way. I think some of his smell got on me."

"It's your smell now."

My father is a handsome, weather-beaten Libertarian with bristly gray hair and a genius IQ. Generally speaking, the human race leaves a bad taste in his mouth. I cannot look at him tonight and see anything other than the father of a student of a sexual abuser. To stare into his face is to stare into a report card of my progress through life. This is not his fault. It's biology. We're destined to compete with each other over the shared turf of our DNA. After all, one of us must have the final word on what it means to be a Haubner.

I sit at the dinner table with my parents and a pot of herbal tea, wondering if they know. This is now something that every young monk in our community must go through: you must sit your parents down and tell them that the life you seriously disappointed them for is actually quite a bit worse than they'd imagined. Remember that teacher whose praises I couldn't stop singing? You know, the guy I sacrificed my career and making you some grandchildren for? Well, one morning I walked in on his suspicious attendant smelling his fingers. . . .

I retire to my sister Molly's old bedroom, where I'll be staying this week. Pictures Molly painted hang from the walls: a dress-wearing troll that vaguely resembles my niece; a black-and-blue portrait of a thinly mustached man kissing an unremarkable woman. They stare at me out of the corners of their poorly rendered eyes. I turn out the lights. The ceiling is asparkle with glow-in-the-dark stickers, a cosmos of crescent moons and stars. Across the hall is my sister Mary's old room, a paean to girly youth with its field hockey trophies and mauve carpet. I feel bad even stepping foot in there. I make it smell like a middle-aged man, a kind of atmosphere abuse.

Step foot in there I do. That room, with its big desk and warm vibe, becomes my headquarters for the next week. Hell is reading account after personal account on a web archive created to chronicle your teacher's sexual depravity in a room where teams of girls in soccer shorts stare out at you from hand-painted picture frames.

Roshi, what have you done?

Is there even a word for it?

There is. There is. Others, outside our community, they keep using it.

We've always used words like groping, fondling. Funny words.

They use words like abuse, assault.

There is a broad continuum upon which Roshi's students and critics rate his behavior, enlightened teaching being ten, and pathological sexual misconduct being one, with every possible permutation in between. In the past, many of the women who had positive sanzen experiences with Roshi were willing to talk openly about them. The women who had negative experiences usually left our community quietly. When someone doesn't come back you don't get a chance to ask them why. Instead you keep hearing from everyone who has stuck around, including the women, about how great a teacher Roshi is.

Now, finally, the other women are getting a chance to speak.

They speak in flat, tortured voices. They speak in that slow, halting, psychologized way common to victims who have rehabilitated their worldview after a collision with some terrible man.

I am not used to hearing people speak this way about my teacher.

Aw, poor Jack. This is all about you, how you feel, huh?

You fucking cunt.

Something is born inside me that absolutely despises what I am. I become what they are calling Roshi, and I become the victim of it, all in the same head. I just stare at the ceiling in my sister Mary's room and let these women radiate off the screen and fill my face until I'm sobbing, often these dry sobs with no tears and a lot of heaving and shaking—*I'm sorry I'm sorry I'm sorry*—and then I crawl down a line into the comments section which is filled with men, this heat and rage, like a jungle-pit that a thousand starving shitting screaming apes have plunged into, and I'm talking at them in my head, beating them off as they swarm me—I never, not once, post anything, not under a fake name, not under my own. That's weird. I don't go there. It all stays in my head.

Then I go downstairs and have dinner with my parents.

They chat about work. Midwestern small talk is better than lithium. So-and-so in shipping sent the wrong gun barrel to Brazil, now it's stuck in customs, and speaking of, did the steel shipment arrive this week, no but the holiday hams did, but then Ungrateful Employee asked if he could give his ham back and get the cash for it instead.

My father gives the final word on the matter. "I hate people." My mother, a small woman with big glasses, cocks her head and considers this, Swiss chocolate in one hand, glass of wine in the other, both vices indulged in in cutely small, nearly homeopathic quantities.

My father retires to the living room, builds a roaring fire in the fireplace he built with his own hands, and watches B-Westerns starring Tom Selleck. "Have you seen this one?" he asks. I have. I saw it last year, when I came home, and the year before that. "Nope," I say. "I've been meaning to, though." "Oh, you're gonna love it," he says. And we watch it together, and it is so bad it makes me feel good, as though its awfulness has numbed my very capacity to discriminate. We consume pretzels and whiskey and I fall into a couch coma as Tom Selleck and his mustache fill the screen.

Roshi impregnated me and pressured me into an abortion. . . . Roshi was impotent his whole fifty years in America. . . . He hit ninety-one and that was it, he couldn't get it up anymore. . . . She may have been seventeen. . . . There was a call to a rape crisis line. . . . He helped me work through my sexual trauma—I would have committed suicide without Roshi. . . . He told me that he would not teach me until I touched his penis. . . . He was giving me a private dharma talk and squeezing my bicep, and I realized, Oh my God he thinks it's my breast—that was when I knew, This isn't sexual, it was never sexual. . . . He spent ten years trying to reach up my hakama skirt, and then he looked me in the eye and denied ever trying to touch me. Lying about this subject has become natural for him and it is something that he's teaching us. . . . I think he was just trying to push my buttons—that's what a Zen master does, and it worked miracles for me. . . . I am convinced now that he used the teachings solely to prey on women. . . . I think he used everything to teach—including his compulsions. . . . Roshi has two children by two different women in Japan, and I'm pretty sure he has more children by students here. . . . I asked Roshi and he said no, they're not his kids. . . . I asked Roshi and he said yes, they're his kids.

Tom Selleck and his stallion leap over a bespectacled husband and wife as they huddle in their Model T, its wheels spinning in a mud puddle. This is meant to symbolize the spirit of the primitive but virile cowboy over the mechanized ethos of modernity, which is wiping out the Wild West and the brawny bros who tamed it. Strong men are a dying breed, the movie tells us. I look over at my old man. These films have been shaping his worldview since he was a little boy. I became a monk to become a different kind of man, a less violent one, someone more like Roshi. But men are the same everywhere, and perhaps I merely exchanged the cowboy archetype for the samurai—the Wild West for the Wild East.

The movie ends and we sit in silence as the fire pops. "When you were a kid, I always thought you were kind of a, how can I put it . . . *lost soul*. You were always looking for people's approval," my father says.

"Are you happy?" he asks.

I nod as though casually considering this. What I'm really doing is scrambling for an answer.

Here's what I'm thinking:

I am part of the diseased now, the culturally repugnant. I am what happens when the world is done listening to you, when the chickens have come home to roost. I'm a straight white middle-class American man on the wrong side of history—the patriarchy.

2. My Apology

I remember the summer that Roshi's sexual behavior went from being a problem that I was struggling with to a problem that I was a part of. I was the shika, or head monk, at the monastery. We had just finished morning sanzen, or koan practice, during a retreat. Normally I would have gone down to the dining hall for formal breakfast—no time to pause, no break in the schedule, one event flowing seamlessly into the next. But I had a question for Roshi about the koan text for his public *teisho* talk that day, so I ran back to his cabin.

Lizzie had already entered his room from her cabin, the two structures connected by a rat-turd-speckled indoor walkway. Roshi was sitting in his chair, looking, as he always did after three hours of koan practice, like an old man who'd just given birth—fleshy, pink, exhausted, glowing with expelled life. Lizzie was on her knees in front of him, clutching his hand in hers, pointing to it and shouting. Hardcore shit was happening. My writer's antenna shot up.

Later Lizzie told me that she had accidentally glanced through the window during sanzen and seen a nun sitting on Roshi's lap.

"What were you doing with his hand when I came in the room?" I asked.

"Smelling his fucking fingers."

The words in her mouth put the stink in my nose. This shit was happening on my watch.

Lizzie and I worked in tandem as inji and shika that summer. We knew each other's moves like a professional dance pair, with Lizzie usually taking the lead. Now forty-two, she'd spent most of her thirties teaching English in Kyoto, where she was "escaping a bad marriage to a worthless and violent piece of shit, not that you asked." She was raised in Georgia and spoke nearly fluent Japanese with a Southern accent. "*Arigatou gozaimasu*, y'all! I'm Japanese at heart. I get the country, I get the people, but I'm too dang tall for those tearoom doorways." She showed me a picture once. She was kneeling on a tatami mat in a traditional kimono, which looked like a miniskirt on her. "The whole country's like one big, tiny-statured family. And clean! I watched a woman take her husband's handkerchief and mop her dog's urine off the sidewalk. If Roshi ever dies, which ain't likely, I'm going back."

For years I'd heard rumors about Roshi's sexual behavior during sanzen, but it wasn't until Lizzie sat me down that night and explained it in detail that I finally understood. Men are visual, technical creatures, and we can be deeply stupid when we feel that it's in our best interests. We need to see Roshi's hand slipping into the ventilation slit sewn into the armpit of your robes. We need to hear him say "Manifest true love" as he pulls you into his lap.

Roshi's age had reached numerical digits normally associated with a full-blown Fahrenheit fever. He had collapsed discs, heart stents, legs that no longer worked, savage arthritis, unremitting sciatica pain, a mouth full of dental implants, and a penis that was buried mangina style in a flab of old man crotch fat like the largely useless organ it was supposed to be at his age.

Smelling his fingers? My 103-year-old teacher had what in college we used to call the stinky pinky?

While in retrospect I see that it was not nearly enough, Lizzie and I worked hard that summer to let female students know that they could come to us if they had problems with Roshi. Lizzie told an unhappy housewife something like, "You can't go into Roshi's room like some confused and horny old woman with her unloved tits hanging out of her robes, you hear me? He'll reflect that back to you every single time. Go in there like an adult. Slap his hand away, tell him 'I don't need no lonely shriveled old man, I got that at home. I need the teaching!'"

The student sobbed. "I just didn't know I could say no to Roshi."

"NO is also love. Roshi taught me that. You can say no all day long, hon," Lizzie said. "Let's say it now, together. Nooooo . . ." When the student found her No, her practice transformed.

When I tried to talk with a jewelry artist from Santa Fe, however, she told me that sexuality was a part of her work with Roshi, and that in fact there was a long history in the East of incorporating sexuality into spiritual practice. Didn't she have the right to define one of the most important relationships in her life as she and the other person saw fit? And what the hell did I have to do with it, anyway? I was just another priest telling her what to do with her body.

That shut me up. The problem, I later learned from Lizzie, was that when Roshi had a sexual sanzen with one female student it tended to "get him going," increasing the likelihood that he would initiate sexual sanzens with other students. So it wasn't just about your personal practice with Roshi. What you did in that room affected other women, women who may or may not have been okay with a 103-year-old Zen master, who resembled an enormous Asian Cabbage Patch Doll, coming at them with his stinky pinky.

What a fucking mess.

That summer I discussed the "Roshi problem" with just about everyone, it seemed, but Roshi. Dutch, a former bodyguard and onetime Ultimate Frisbee coach, came to town. I took him out for Thai.

"Why do you think I left the monastery years ago?" he roared. "In protest of Roshi's sexual shenanigans!"

"I thought you were kicked out for putting a wooden tofu hammer through a window."

"That is outrageous! It wasn't a hammer, it was my fist."

I asked him about an infamous meeting where several oshos confronted Roshi on this issue. Did one osho really threaten to punch another? As factions formed, did Roshi really admit "I have a woman problem"? At one point did Roshi really try to bite his tongue off—was there actually blood coming out the sides of his mouth?

"I can't remember," said Dutch. "I'm bad with details."

"Roshi goes too far."

"Where is too far? Is it a place, an idea? Can I get there by train?"

"Do you think Roshi's enlightened?"

"I don't think him being enlightened means he ain't gonna have problems. Everyone has karma. For me the question is, Does Roshi's karma bother him?" He told me the story about the rape he suffered at the hands of his mother. "I've consciously forgiven her, but there is some part of me that won't heal in this lifetime. It comes out. It colors everything. Everyone—even Roshi—has a shadow side. I think Roshi is somebody who can roll with his own shadow and roll with your shadow. That was my experience of the guy. And everyone forgives him his shadow because he forgives you your shadow. Roshi's got the goods, even if he's a little bad."

"Just a little?"

"This is your koan, little buddy, and it's the koan of a lifetime. The Christians ask, How can bad things happen to good people? Well, how can good people manifest bad things?"

At the end of the summer, Roshi held a *zadankai*, which was basically public koan practice, sort of a Q and A on steroids. Things got off to a brisk start. He poked a tattooed student with his walking stick—"Where are you?!" The student collapsed into a lazy grin. "I dislike your beard!" Roshi cried.

He spun to a veteran of the latest Iraq war. "Where are *you*?" The student threw his glasses at Roshi. Lizzie translated Roshi's sputtering reply thusly: "You gotta be kidding me!"

Roshi clapped and sang. We clapped and sang. A man with long stringy hair, a haunted old soul, said, "I see a baby, I cry. When someone is suffering, I suffer. Is this wrong?"

We were two hours in. Things were unraveling.

"*Jikan des*," I told Roshi. Time's up.

My job. To set boundaries.

He asked, "Are there any more questions?" He asked again.

He turned to me. "Shika! Question?"

I did not plan to ask him anything. It just slipped out.

"Some people think sanzen is all about sex . . ."

Nervous laughter filled the room.

"Other people think sanzen has nothing to do with sex. What is the middle way between these two views?"

Lizzie translated.

A look of surprise and then rage crossed Roshi's face—"The same look Dad used to flash before he hit me," I wrote in my journal.

"This is a really important question. Whoever asks it should stand right here and say it to my face," Roshi said.

This was a challenge to move away from the theoretical "some people think," and to directly manifest my own truth before him. If ever there was a moment to confront Roshi, this was it.

Instead, I stayed silent.

I thought about that silence a lot as I sat in my sister Mary's bedroom the Thanksgiving that the scandal broke. How many women had been inappropriately touched—or worse—by Roshi during my time as head monk? I read a short comment on a Zen blog from Sandy: "Two people went into sanzen, Roshi and the student. But the monks only really cared about one of them."

I hadn't seen Sandy since that summer, when I accepted her as a student at the monastery. Though twenty-four-years-old, she was built like a tween with her own Disney series, which is to say that certain things about her were very big—her eyes, her lips, her imagination—while other things were very small—her fingernails, her nose, her tolerance for assholes. Once I asked her for feedback on a poem I'd written. She read it and said, "You are an exceedingly lonely man." Somehow this made me feel less lonely.

Sandy was another in a long list of platonic friendships that I have nurtured during dry spells where I've concluded that a real relationship involving oral sex and Netflix nights is just way too much work. One day, she was monopolizing my lunch break to tell me about an ex-boyfriend, and as I tried to break free so that I could go back to my cabin to jerk off to her, she let slip a comment about sanzen that lodged in my spine like a sliver of ice.

"Sandy, before you came here, when you were studying with Helmut in Connecticut, did he warn you about Roshi?"

I assumed she knew what this meant.

"Yes," she said.

"And everything's okay in sanzen?"

She paused. We weren't supposed to talk about sanzen.

At this point I feel like I need to explain a little of the history behind sanzen, or koan practice, which has been passed down for centuries by the fiercest and most realized Zen masters. Honestly, though, I'd rather you just Google it if you're interested. I, for one, knew nothing about koan practice when I started Zen. I just figured it was a pretext to interact with a Zen master, with a whole lot of Japanese attention to form piled on top.

Roshi never gave me a classic koan like "What is the sound of one hand clapping," or "What did your original face look like before your parents were born?" Instead, in my first sanzen meeting he asked me, "Where are you?" Later, I returned to his cabin and repeated the question back to him as I understood it.

"Where is Roshi?"

"Ha ha ha! Roshi know where Roshi is. Where are *you*?"

We went on like this for weeks. I tried everything. I didn't know much about koan practice, but I did know this: you don't typically answer a koan verbally. Imagine that your spouse asks, "Do you love me?" A good answer is yes. A better answer is a demonstration of your love. You meet her question with a manifestation so complete that there is nothing left to be said. You give your heart instead of talking about how you feel. This is the kind of commitment required to answer a koan.

"I need 100 percent," Roshi always told me. "Not 50 percent, not 90 percent, 100 percent!"

I never really did answer my first koan. I exhausted myself trying, and then Roshi gave me my next koan. That night I went into sanzen with a typically wild gimmick that probably involved shouting and doing an interpretive dance while making strange faces. Zen isn't an intellectual discipline, but it isn't bad performance art either. Roshi laughed for about, I swear to God, ten minutes.

Then he said, "Be. More. Normal."

Before I could reply, both of his hands were holding mine. He pulled me close and bowed until our foreheads were touching.

He said, "Your heart. My heart. Same."

We stayed like that for a tiny eternity. It felt like he was taking the weight of my life off my shoulders. I was so relaxed I began to shake, as though some tension buried deep in my bone marrow had found release. When we parted he looked in my eyes.

"True Love important."

I knew exactly what he meant, and he gave me my next koan.

No one can give you an answer to a koan. You must discover it for yourself. That is why Zen masters forbid their students to talk about sanzen. An air of intrigue surrounded that tiny cabin where your teacher met with your peers. It was a black box—students went in and came out, and you had no idea what went on inside. If you lived at the monastery, Zen practice was the most important thing in your life, and the majority of monks considered sanzen to be the most important part of their Zen practice. And so we had a situation where an astonishing amount of energy and mystery was built up around a group activity that everyone did privately with one man, and no one talked about.

Fertile ground for profound Zen practice—and open secrets.

When I asked Sandy how her sanzen was going with Roshi that afternoon, I was crossing a line.

"Roshi is teaching me about True Love," she said.

This may have been a tacit invitation to ask her another question. It may have been a polite way of telling me that the conversation was over. With Sandy you never could tell.

I chose to leave it at that.

A few weeks later Sandy told me that she was leaving the monastery even though she'd paid for the whole summer. When I asked her why, she gave me a gift. I kept it in my parents' attic. I climbed the dusty attic stairs and retrieved a small box. Inside was a homemade flipbook (Sandy's specialty). It featured an angry little stick figure getting a very animated erection that grew bigger and bigger until, in the final pages, it popped like balloon. The stick figure stood there with a frown and a gaping hole where his penis used to be.

"Very artistic," I'd told her.

"Do you understand?" she'd asked.

I put the flipbook back in the cardboard box, took the box downstairs to the fireplace, and set it on the hot coals. As I watched it burn I couldn't stop thinking about that angry stick figure with a huge hole where his manhood should have been. I remembered something Dutch once told me.

"Roshi abuses the women and emasculates the men."

It was quiet in the house. The grandfather clock on the wall had long ago stopped ticking. I tried to meditate, but all I could do was think. That summer, after the zadankai, I gave a talk on wisdom and compassion as being like the beating wings that float your heart. If wisdom means giving yourself to something greater than yourself, compassion means giving yourself to something smaller or more vulnerable than yourself. "Both are equally necessary," I said.

Sandy came up to me afterward, put her fingers on my chest, and pushed. "I wish you could walk it like you talk it."

"I'm a writer," I said. "For me talking *is* walking."

"Oh, really? Why didn't you say anything earlier when Roshi challenged you to speak your truth about sex and sanzen? What kind of a writer are you? Some day," she said, "you need to tell the whole truth about Roshi."

Spread out on the desk in my sister Mary's room were the publisher's galleys for *Zen Confidential: Confessions of a Wayward Monk*. Concurrent with the scandal was the deadline for the final edits on my first book. Aside from being too long and filled with a bizarrely high number of poop jokes and portmanteaus, the book portrayed Roshi in an entirely positive light. I came close to showing his dark side in the final chapter, but then I balked. Instead, I focused on my love for Roshi and the light he's shown in my life—true, all of it, but as the saying goes, a truth is something whose opposite is also true.

I called my mentor. "I have to tell the whole truth about Roshi."

"You're not a good enough writer."

"I'm going to add a chapter."

"Uh-oh."

"It's about the time Roshi, Lizzie, and I visited her Mom in Atlanta."

"When Roshi lost his temper?"

"Yes."

"Don't change your book. It's beautiful the way it is. Look . . . write. Just write. That's how you process things. But don't rewrite your book. Write a letter to the women who were harmed. Write an apology."

It came out pretty quickly. It was an exorcism.

Everything clicked when I realized whom I was writing to.

I wanted to tell Sandy that I was sorry for my role in her suffering—when she came out of the sanzen room, I wasn't there for her. No one was. I wanted to acknowledge the truth of her experience, whatever it was, on her terms.

I believed that if we faced the absolute worst in our teacher, it would bring out the best in us: the women who were harmed might have a shot at healing, and our community could finally move into a post-Roshi world free of his mistakes. This, I felt, was a necessary step in our evolution from a sangha that was completely dependent on one man, to a mature collective of practitioners who could take care of themselves, and each other.

It seemed almost too perfect. Nine months earlier, I'd watched as Roshi turned every external indication that he was dying from aspiration pneumonia—gagging on his phlegm, for example—into a spiritual practice: consciously, repetitively, coughing pints of phlegm into Kleenexes, and then repeating a few Buddhist phrases over and over. Why had he fought so hard, at 105 years of age, to come back from the dead?

He had one last piece of unfinished business.

And now we who loved him so much could come into ourselves as his living legacy and help him finish whatever wretched karma he'd brought into this life, that had cast such a long shadow over his otherwise luminous work. I had absolute faith that the good Roshi did far outweighed the bad, and that once we passed through the scandal, this truth would come to light. Roshi had taught us to never turn away from anything—and so this was the ultimate challenge, the final koan: to face the paradox, the darkness in our enlightened master.

The morning I flew back to LA, my parents took me to Perk Place, a homey little café where the bathroom walls are stenciled with wry inspirational quotes by famous thinkers.

I told them everything.

My mother looked at me from across the table as hand-painted writers—Hemingway, Shakespeare, Poe—stared at me from the walls. Precision instrument parenting—I'd never appreciated it until now. A Midwestern specialty. They let you be, very carefully giving you space to come out of your shell, but never pushing you. At no point did my mother shift uncomfortably, or jam up the flow of words with a question or frown. She just received what I was saying. It was like I could talk right through her, I could release everything.

"Well, that was serious," my father said.

"I mean on some level I gotta hand it to the guy," he told me in the car ride to the airport. "These were all adult women, right?"

"Let's hope so."

"Yeah, on some level, I really gotta hand it to the guy."

Life goes on, I thought.

"This always happens, all the women make eyes at the cult leader and then they're shocked when he starts grabbin' their knockers—not of course that you're in a cult or anything!"

I'd always thought that my parents didn't accept my way of life as a monk. What they weren't, however, was impressed by it—which is what I'd wanted. I'd wanted them to say "We thought we raised you correctly, but no, you have ventured forth into the world and found a better way! You are superior to us!" In fact, rain or shine—heady monastic insights, or a hideous sex scandal—they loved me just the same, a love as flat, peaceful, and perennial as the brown cornfields whizzing past my window on the way to Mitchell International Airport.

3. We Live in the Age of the Internet (and That Age Is Five)

I floated my apology to a few trusted oshos. They floated it to a few more. Suddenly it was out there, and the responses started pouring in. If I had to share just one single piece of wisdom with you that I have gained from this sex scandal, it would be:

Never hit reply all.

I remember one e-mail that I sent to at least sixty people—I mean everyone from board members to an ailing nun to a world-famous singer/songwriter—that started, "Dear ____ , In the words of Paul Newman, you got a way of starting conversations that end conversation...."

There was a lot of that.

E-mail is a great way to communicate about complex, intimate issues with large numbers of people like the electric chair is the perfect place to sit down and take a load off. From five-thousand-word diatribes written by senior oshos complete with italics, boldface, and several font styles, to a nun's vicious and bizarre one-liners with no caps and no punctuation, like rusty little needles of prose spit off the screen into your eyeball. Nobody was at their best.

Outside of Roshi there was no real authority in our community. There was a kind of pecking order, with oshos at the top, and there was an unspoken hierarchy among the oshos based on experience, insight, and temple size. But here's the problem with an unspoken hierarchy: those at the top of it are too humble and cautious to take charge, and those at the bottom of it are too stupid to know their place. The result—and this was the problem with so much of the discussion on the Internet about Roshi—was that the loudest, most persistent voices usually prevailed.

My apology did not apply to all of the oshos, and so not all of the oshos felt they could sign it. Some didn't feel complicit in Roshi's misconduct, some felt that there was no misconduct, some felt that the apology didn't go far enough in addressing the misconduct, and some felt that staying silent was the best response. I felt a stab in my stomach every time my phone buzzed. When the latest e-mail arrived I'd never read it, I'd just speed skim to get the general feel and then quickly bury it in my "Crisis" folder and argue in my head with the person who'd sent it.

We were trying to have a nice night off, me and the monks. We were at a theater on the Third Street Promenade watching *Silver Linings Playbook* with Jennifer Lawrence, and my phone was buzzing like an angry little dildo, and I just had to look—if I didn't I wouldn't be able to enjoy the rest of the movie knowing that a fresh diatribe was waiting for me, so I actually put the phone under my sweater and then pulled my sweater up over my head and opened the e-mail and it was from the Zen student sitting next to me in the theater—

"Dude. Stop it. Enjoy the film."

A couple oshos rewrote my apology. They rewrote it some more. It began to resemble a parody of itself, like a Beverly Hills housewife who keeps going under the knife. My mentor sent out an e-mail decrying e-mail and insisting that we all meet in person. My apology shrunk to a few paragraphs announcing that the oshos would gather after the holidays to discuss the allegations.

Both the *New York Times* and the *Los Angeles Times* decided to hold off on publishing their articles about Roshi until after our meeting. The story was swelling to international proportions. It spoke to our cultural moment, with women in all walks of life now using the Internet to fight back against powerful men who had sexually harassed or abused them. Around the world, Buddhists and non-Buddhists alike were waiting to hear what we would say.

This is when I began to lose sleep. When I started smoking heavily. When I caught myself in self-conversation in front of other people. I stopped bathing. My sex drive went cold, though I didn't stop masturbating, which is a creepy, pleasureless feeling. I lost weight. I lost my temper. I began to forget things—my Internet passwords, how to tie my osho belt, why I walked into a room.

I was haunted by the faceless, hysterical voices of the Internet; by the hate e-mails piling up in the office inbox, each of which I tried to respond to, which only made the haters angrier; by the man who called late one night from Greece and told me a wild and improbable story about Roshi and his sister—I listened and listened and I really thought we were getting somewhere, and then he threatened me personally, or at least I think he threatened me.

I'll never forget this—it was 2:00 a.m., I had to be up in an hour as we were in the middle of a retreat, and so I was overworked and beyond exhausted, but I was nodding and agreeing and trying to get inside this guy's head and empathize with him, when his voice dropped and out of nowhere he whispered:

"I'm gonna cunt you."

"I understand," I said, going on pure momentum.

"Did you hear me?"

"Wait, what?"

"I'm gonna cunt you."

I tried to politely correct him. "Cut me?"

"Cunt you."

I tried to argue with him for a little bit from the semantic angle, reiterating that he probably wanted to cut me, as cunting me made no sense, but no, he assured me that what he really wanted more than anything was to cunt me, preferably right in my cunt, and then he hung up. It was a sign of the times that I reviewed the conversation in my head for several moments, wondering where it went wrong. Perhaps I should have just let him run with his vaginal verbing thing. Who was I to question cunting? If it was real to him, that was all that mattered, and I needed to respect that.

An older monk, a nun, and I planned the osho meeting. We found an American Roshi from another lineage who had been through a similar scandal with her teacher. She agreed to moderate the meeting, which was bound to be contentious. Meanwhile, the more I learned about sexual misconduct as a crime and a pathology, the more I began to see it everywhere—including in myself.

When someone you love is at the heart of a sex scandal, you inevitably awaken in a cold sweat thinking, *Wasn't there that one time?* The Catholic girlfriend, that rainy afternoon. Did you ask for consent? No one asked for consent back then, are you kidding me? *May I spread your labia just so? I'm sorry, I didn't hear you, can you use your outside voice?* You touched her when she wasn't in the mood. Remember? But she never said no, right? It was just a feeling you got. You dated her for five years and never had actual intercourse. You were both so chaste, so loving. So why does this one rainy afternoon stand out?

Every man has vaginal blood on his hands.

So I did what men do when they feel guilty. I went after someone else and tried to punish him for the same sin. I hammered my mentor who, I felt, was a little too forgiving of Roshi, and himself.

"I'm sorry, but you're gay, you've never had a girlfriend—you don't understand women at all," I straightsplained.

"I understand them enough to know that you hate them," he said.

"I don't hate women, *you* hate women."

"No, YOU hate women."

"You hate women as only a gay man can—with *indifference*."

"Well you're not gay, forty, unmarried, and bitter about it—do the math, Misogyny-boy!"

Then there were those things I secretly thought and felt but could not say—because I, like you, feel and think everything, especially if it's inappropriate.

Like:

Seeing your true nature is not an easy or pat process, and perhaps it includes running up against something in your teacher that you really don't want to see—like his cock. Maybe Roshi was willing to go there with you, not as a "teaching," but almost as a kind of beast, a threshold guardian standing between you and the insight that your true self is beyond good and bad, male and female, and all other binary distinctions. In real Zen practice, not this bullshit you're going to get at your drop-in mindfulness class at the hot-yoga center, you have to face your demons. So, was the problem really all with Roshi, or are you projecting at least some of your issues and history with men onto him and "the patriarchy" because that's easier than taking full responsibility for yourself? Don't think that just because feminism has the cultural advantage right now that it doesn't also have a shadow.

And then there were the women in our community who were a bit too furious in their declarations of loyalty to Roshi. Let's be clear: you don't have decades of sexualized Zen practice going on in a community like ours without serious buy-in from any number of women. When the scandal broke these women had to look at themselves, and maybe some of them didn't like what they saw. If they questioned Roshi now, they had to question the years of decisions that they'd made under his influence—they had to go back to that first time that he touched them and they decided to run with it. What if they'd chosen differently?

And what about the men who had conspired, consciously or not, to keep Roshi's behavior at the level of an open secret all these years? They were almost comically inarticulate now, as though their tongues had been damaged by what they'd always known but never spoken of. But it was more than their tongues that were damaged. If no one talks about something that everybody knows is happening, then each and every person must bear the whole burden of the collective secret him- or herself. What began as a problem becomes a nightmare that turns, without outside intervention, into a demon. At that point the problem is released from the individual back out into the community. The repressed problem is taking its revenge.

An argument can be made that Roshi's sexual behavior was, on a one-on-one basis, extremely helpful to certain individuals. It taught them openness and egoless intimacy, and to trust themselves and to let go of their hang-ups. The problem, in my experience, was that this behavior invariably came back to affect our community as a whole in toxic ways. It's like an affair within a family. A husband cheats on his wife with a married coworker. The experience may be beautiful and transformative for the two of them, but chances are it will double back on their families in devastating ways. Without passing judgment on the couple you can still see that their behavior has serious consequences.

That's what we're talking about. Not right, wrong; pure, impure; he said, she said. We're talking about actions and consequences.

A famous Zen story asks, Is an enlightened person subject to cause and effect? The answer: He cannot ignore it.

By the time the meeting arrived I was a chain-smoking, over-caffeinated insomniac ready to explode with self-righteous male-bitch anger. In other words, I was in a perfect state to discuss sensitive issues regarding sexual misconduct with a bunch of other mostly bepenised priests.

Of the meeting itself, what can I say? Not much. We all agreed to a confidentiality statement. Sometimes it felt like *Game of Thrones* in a monastery with all the parts played by the Three Stooges. Other times it felt like a loving family cleaning out a very old wound. We'd always been pretty good at sitting in silence together, but we'd never sat down and talked about our problems and feelings. Monks shared things that I will take to my grave.

At the end of the weekend something special happened. Not only did we agree to hire a neutral third party to reach out to the women who'd been harmed, but a version of my old apology resurfaced. An osho had brought a hard copy of it with him on the plane. He read it aloud, and the oshos present voted to release it as a statement. We were finally able to put our differences aside and speak with one voice.

Naturally, the good vibes were short-lived.

4. Death of the Charismatic Teacher

The *New York Times* piece came out while we were in retreat. I was scrambling forty eggs on the stove grill when a monk the size of an NBA power forward burst through the kitchen door—"You oshos pissed in the sky, and now it's raining down on all of us," the dharmasaur roared.

I had to admit, it was a pretty good line. I wanted to tell him, "It's more like Roshi ejaculated into the sky and now it's raining down on us," but sometimes you just have to let people vent. And vent they did. Many outside of our community responded warmly to the osho letter. I'm told that a copy exists at the Berkeley Law Library as a model for a formal apology. Women who'd been harmed by Roshi and our community said that with the osho letter they knew they'd finally been heard—these were the women I'd written the thing for.

However, there were those (especially in the online Zen scene) for whom the apology simply served as verification of their worst criticisms of our community. That hurt—we bowed our heads and they kicked us in the nuts. And it wasn't just the outside world that had been waiting to hear what we oshos would say. Our dharma brothers and sisters, Roshi's students, had been waiting, too. Many felt that the apology gave the press carte blanche to print whatever they wanted about Roshi.

"Your apology validated every lie, half-truth, and rumor that's out there. You threw Roshi under the bus to save your own reputations."

"I read that apology and I thought, 'Wow, thanks guys. You basically called Roshi a sexual deviant. So what does that make me, a nun who studied with him for thirty-six years? A slut!'"

"For years while I dealt with this problem you ignored me, or told me that Roshi was trying to teach me something, or said that women shouldn't study Zen anyway, and then when I finally made peace with Roshi touching me you turned around and told the whole world that he'd been abusing me all along!"

"I never once felt abused by Roshi. He loved me unconditionally. I feel abused by your apology letter!"

"If what you wrote in that apology is true then you oshos were either negligent in your duty to protect new students, or complicit in their abuse. Either way you should hand in your robes and resign from your temples."

"I'm glad the women who felt that Roshi abused them have found their voice, but now the women who felt that Roshi helped them have *lost theirs*."

Still others felt that the apology didn't go far enough in its condemnation of Roshi, or they decided that with the release of the osho statement they now had some closure on their time in our community, and could move on. Board members resigned, monks handed in their robes, priests publically disaffiliated from our organization.

Through it all, Roshi stayed silent. He was still the spiritual figurehead of our community, not to mention the chief abbot of our LA temple (a largely titular role by this point), but the scandal, not to mention old-age-induced simplicity (his spirit was bright and clear, but his mind was no longer razor sharp), put his status in extremely tricky territory.

A fresh round of rumors started online that Roshi was still fully in charge of the organization. Roshi isn't even in charge of his own bowel movements, I thought. The truth was, no one was in charge of our organization, and there wasn't even really an organization to speak of. We were a loving but loosely affiliated group of fellow practitioners spread out over the world. For decades Roshi had called the shots at his four main training centers, where he did the bulk of his teaching, but after he'd gotten sick nine months before the scandal broke, he'd stopped making decisions, appointed no new leadership, and gone into retirement without a single word on the future of our community. Many of us were holding out hope that he was about to appoint a new Roshi, or at least describe some sort of succession plan.

After the osho meeting there was to be a change in management at the head temple in LA. The old shika was going back to Poland. He knelt across from Saisho, the new shika. Saisho told me that his only purpose was "to serve Roshi and the sangha," but I caught a whiff of spiritual ambition in his decision to leave his temple in Santa Cruz and come to LA, a city he despised. Good for him! I thought. Saisho could light up a room with his words and presence. Tall, tough, and Jewish, he had a degree from Princeton, where he broke his nose three times after joining the boxing club, which was "a bit heavy on angry gentiles." Myotai, Saisho's sister, was a devoted and strong-willed osho who ran Buddha Field, one of Roshi's main training centers. She and Saisho were stalwarts in our community.

A humidifier purred, spitting wet dust into the morning sunbeams. Roshi sat in his black leather chair as Saisho read a report about the osho meeting. Lizzie translated and I poured everyone green tea. What's black and white and loved all over? Lucy, the temple cat. She was lounging uneasily at Roshi's feet. Unfortunately this refreshingly uncontroversial sangha member had leukemia. She was at the stage where she kept puking up clots of blood. She often delivered these blood-marbled barf babies at Roshi's feet.

I watched her, waiting for it . . .

Saisho finished his report, which included a request for money to hire a neutral third party to mediate between our organization and the women who had been harmed. The room was nearly womb temperature, and a satellite clock ticked with metronomic regularity. Lizzie kept snatching fruit flies out of the air with one hand. Roshi said something to her and me. She translated.

"Thank you for putting this problem on the table and taking responsibility. Because I am old, I cannot."

Roshi agreed that the head temple should supply the funds for the neutral receivers of harm. He was talking to Lizzie and me only. This was becoming increasingly common. Communication with the rare visitor had to be brokered through the two of us, mostly Lizzie, for Roshi spoke almost no English now. He seemed especially tired this morning. His eyes were closed and he leaned on his fist. The skin on his face, so loose, was draped over his knuckles. He needed a shave. After a stretch of silence it became clear that he'd drifted to sleep midsentence.

Saisho got up to leave. "Thank you, Roshi."

Roshi's eyes shot open. He spun on Saisho and started jabbing his finger at him and shouting. Lizzie tried to translate but couldn't keep up with this detailed assault on Saisho's character. I'd seen Roshi's anger flash up like this before—the morning we visited Lizzie's mother in Atlanta.

The blood left Saisho's face. He just sat there, his broad shoulders hunched. Another monk had told me, Saisho doesn't know the difference between surrender and submission.

Roshi switched to English: "You—your sister—me. Old thinking! Old thinking! *Our way, over!*"

At one point during the scandal Roshi had wanted to apologize in person to any woman who felt harmed by him, but for various reasons this never happened. Instead, he went into *sange,* or repentance, for the rest of his life, and he wrote out a short apology. It was never made public, and I only remember two lines: "I made too many mistakes. Trying to teach is already a mistake."

A Zen patriarch's greatest responsibility is to train and anoint a worthy successor so that the living wisdom of the tradition is passed on, like the flame from one candle to the next. Saisho was widely perceived as being one of Roshi's top oshos—a brilliant Buddhist thinker, a dedicated teacher, and a fierce practitioner.

Roshi was always tough on his older students, but I'd never seen him so clearly dismiss Saisho and his entire generation. If the old way was over, what had they been doing all these years, and who would lead our sangha in the future?

Later, when I asked Roshi this, he said, "You're not a boy anymore!"

There would be no successor. This meant that Roshi's spiritual bloodline would end with him. Technically speaking, his unique strain of Zen would perish.

No more patriarchs.

This was Roshi's third death: the death of his lineage.

5. Opposites Attack

Sex scandals suck. They suck the air out of the room, the life out of your practice, and the hope out of your heart. You lose weight, shit blood, and sob and sob until the bone structure of your face begins to change.

Plus, you talk on the phone a lot. It's midnight and I have a 4:00 a.m. wake-up. I'm at our LA temple, pacing through a dark and moldy back bedroom (the cheese cave, we call it). Saisho has already left LA and moved back to Santa Cruz. I picture him sitting in the shadows in his impressive Buddhist library, puffing on his vape rig and jabbing his finger at me.

"Roshi has a demon side—a demon side! And I want this sangha to face it! I want this sangha to face his demon!"

A demon is a problem that has soaked in darkness for so long that it's taken on a life of its own. I pass by a mirror. *You've caught this demon yourself. Have you faced it?*

For reasons ultimately known only to him, Roshi wants Myotai, Saisho's sister, to retire from her role as shika of Buddha Field, a post she's held for twenty-five years. The backlash in our community to the osho apology letter has found its culmination in a letter of support for Roshi's decision to demand Myotai's resignation. Eighteen monks and nuns, known in the increasingly purple Internet coverage of our family squabble as "the gang of eighteen," have signed it.

I do not agree with or support this letter.

Lizzie does.

After I get off the phone with Saisho, I try to shout his point of view across to her—to deliver the demon now inside me.

"At some point you're gonna have to turn off the phone and figure out where the hell you stand," she says.

"I stand with a foot on both sides, can't you see this?"

When it comes to her own experience, Lizzie has made peace with Roshi's sexual behavior. "When I first became his student I was really confused," she explains. "I was like, Is this okay? Is this True Love? Because he'd say 'No thinking, no talking,' and it felt like True Love when you were huggin' the guy. I mean, I was still hurting real bad from my divorce back then. So things would, you know, escalate and he'd go to a place that was a little more intimate. He'd pull me in and whisper in Japanese, 'You aren't supposed to do this.' I should've pushed his hand away from day one, but I went with it. I was curious about the process. I was looking for True Love. I was really curious, I wanted to see where it would lead."

"Where could it possibly lead?"

"Some women are like, 'I really learned how to feel again in sanzen.' They've got issues with their husbands, that's why they go to Roshi, he'll present intimacy in a way that's beyond your normal understanding. There's something real in there that you could explore with him, but I have mixed feelings about it. You could explore, sure, but ultimately that's just not my way. I went through a short period of exploring, then it became an issue for me—*This is not why I came here, to fool around with this old man.* So, one day I bowed and sat in front of him and said, 'ROSHI! I'm serious about this practice, please take me seriously! I'm here to do Zen.'"

Her position on Roshi's sexual behavior has evolved since that summer when I caught her smelling his fingers. "Hon, I used to be standing in your boots—unclear and full of fear. I don't judge

Roshi anymore. I think his wisdom is way deeper than his mistakes, so it all shakes out in the end." She taps her head. "We have a saying in the South: Keep the worms outta your apple. Don't let guys like Saisho get into your head. You talk talk talk on the phone all day, collecting opinions instead of living your own damn truth."

"I listen to other people! I let people in, Lizzie."

"I beg to differ, and I would know."

"I always try and see both sides, you know that."

I completely honor Lizzie's experience. I also completely honor Myotai's experience. After the scandal broke, she came to me with tears in her eyes. She told me how at age twenty-six she rode west in her rusty VW Bug to give her life to Roshi and Zen practice. "I was just a girl. I did not know anything. I trusted Roshi." I realized then how complex the problem was: those like Myotai and Saisho, who were among the most complicit in the abuse of power and sex in our community, were also victims of that same abuse.

Myotai infamously said, "Sleeping with the teacher is the fast track to enlightenment." That she is now, during this sex scandal, being asked to resign her position of leadership feels to many of us like an appropriate request long overdue—that it is coming from the man who is at the center of this scandal is irrelevant to some, absurd to others, and infuriating to Saisho.

He is taking a public stand against Roshi. It is not easy for him, and he is not wearing the struggle well. Something has collapsed in his heart, and you can see it in his face, in his sunken chapped cheeks and darting eyes. No one admires Roshi more than he does, and no one loves Roshi more than his sister.

"We gave our lives to this practice! I raised my son and she raised her girl at Buddha Field! And this is what we get?"

He moved swiftly, getting himself and a lawyer-monk that he ordained on the board of directors at Buddha Field. They now effectively control the center, not Roshi or any of Roshi's representatives.

"Roshi's always had all the power! *All the power!* Not anymore!"
Myotai isn't going anywhere.

And so our community is splitting right down the middle. I want to do something about it, but when you're in a position to make a difference, as I am, this often just means that you have a front-row seat to a disaster in the making that you cannot change, but will be blamed for.

"What do you WANT?" Lizzie screams.

Because the problem is complex, my solution is complex. I want to embrace everyone's point of view, through the teachings that Roshi has transmitted, which are greater than any one of us, including him, but which exclude none of us. He once said: "There are many wonderful things in this world, but the best of all is to hold the whole world together in your hand . . . good things, bad things, life and death, good and evil, everything together."

I want to hold the whole community together, the gang of eighteen as well as Saisho and Myotai, and this is what's running through my head: Roshi hurt people and shamed us. He needs to resign from his role as chief abbot of the head temple and ask for our forgiveness. Then Myotai and Saisho and the rest of us can step forward and ask for forgiveness for our role in the problems that have plagued our community for decades and are tearing us apart now. It all starts at the top, it starts with Roshi. He needs to model humility and surrender, and then Myotai and Saisho on the one side, and the gang of eighteen on the other, can follow his example—as they surely will.

"There are three jewels in Buddhism, right? The Buddha, the Dharma, and the Sangha," I tell Lizzie. "We always valued the Buddha, or teacher—Roshi. And we always valued the dharma, or teachings—Rinzai Zen. But we never truly valued the sangha—each other. Anatta means not only seeing that you have no fixed, abiding self, but that others have no fixed, abiding self either. The person across from me is empty of my projections. I want nothing from them. I fear nothing about them. I hate nothing in them. I am an extension of them, and they pick up where I leave off. We need each other. We *are* each other. This is sangha. This is True Love. This will replace Roshi. *We* will replace Roshi. But he must step aside first."

"Are you kidding me? Yack yack yack. He's sitting right there. You want him to resign? Tell him yourself!" Lizzie says.

The whole time we've been shouting, Roshi has been slumped in his chair just around the shoji screen. He's deaf, but he's not that deaf. Yet what can he do? He's so old.

I kneel before him.

"Go ahead!" Lizzie says. "Fire away!"

To get through to him, I will need her help. He practically thinks through her now. If she translates but doesn't believe what I'm saying, neither will he. I've seen him burn defiant monks to the core with his anger, and no matter how right I may feel I am, I still need these two. They're all I've got.

We are floating in each others' gaze. If I am going to stand up to Roshi, now is the moment. And yet it is no moment at all. I cannot manifest a truth that is equal to his mistakes. If I could, he would no longer be the Roshi, I would. He's old and he's weak, but that doesn't mean he's vulnerable. He's as solid as ever, and he's not going to change, not now. He is a patriarch to the end. The sangha will never empower itself without his affirmation, and he will never affirm the sangha until it empowers itself.

And so it's over.

I want to tell him everything, but all that comes out is the truth:

"You broke my heart."

"*What?*"

Lizzie thinks this is meant for her. It triggers resentments half a decade old, from back when we were lovers.

"You know, you broke my heart . . . I mean, that was it, I moved on. It was hard, but I moved on. Yet here you are, still in my life, acting like I owe you something. You use me so you can stay close to Roshi and warm your little hands by his fire, but then you don't fully trust Roshi and you ain't got a big enough pair to tell him that, so you lay all your shit on me!"

"I trust Roshi, I just don't want to give him complete and total control over my life—"

"Yeah sure, you want to keep control but take no responsibility. Yeah, that's real Zen. Maybe in your book."

"*I'm* controlling?" I jab my finger at the closed window. "You control every breeze that comes in and out of this room. You're so close to Roshi I can't tell the two of you apart anymore. Decisions are coming out of this room and I don't know who's making them—"

"What the fuck are you saying?"

We are scream-whispering over Roshi, who is huddled beneath us, his bald head lowering into his thick cotton robes like a turtle sinking into its shell. The argument escalates. We are equally matched. She says I have mother issues, and cites why. I point out the divorces in her family and claim that she comes from three generations of women who can't live with men.

"I've been around violent men my whole life, I'm a goddamn expert on the breed. And honey, this sangha is full of them, and you're one of the worst."

"Where do you think we get it from?"

"Blame it on Roshi, aaaalways Roshi's fault. Take some responsibility for once!"

"You're just like Myotai—you support the man in power because it gives you power!"

"I have NO influence over Roshi. I'm just keepin' my head down and doin' my best!"

"You're doing too much. You're trying to control everything."

"You're trying to control me!"

"Because you're controlling Roshi!"

That's when she loses it.

Then I lose it. I raise my fists and the sound of flesh on flesh smacks both of us silent.

6. The Aborted Fetus of the Patriarchy

I get a length of toilet paper.

I open the medicine cabinet over Roshi's sink. It contains a great variety of expensive lotions. All the better for the evening's activities.

I get some lube.

Lizzie is out dancing. After last night's fight, she needs it. She has written detailed instructions on taking care of Roshi. After I'm sure she's gone, I make a point of crumpling them into a ball and tossing them over my shoulder. Then I think twice and carefully uncrumple and smooth the wrinkled paper. Too late. She'll see that I mangled her Roshi Instruction Manual. I must get rid of the evidence. I drop the paper in the toilet, flush.

Oh shit. I actually needed those. I have no idea how to care for Roshi.

He sits on his black chair, feet propped up on a foam square, his wireless headphones connected to the TV, the only way he can hear the sumo match playing. He looks up at the atomic clock. Looks at me. Looks back at the TV. He never appears to be actually watching TV. He just sort of squints, watching TV happen, as I stand there, watching *him* happen. A 105-year-old body is an altar upon which the cosmos publically displays the mortality of our species. Yet there is a tiny pulse of ancient life quivering beneath his white cotton robes and worn-out flesh. This is what I see when I look at him—it is blinding. I turn away.

I lie down on Roshi's bed. The shoji screen separating us gives me some privacy, which is good, because I am going to jerk off. That's right, and there's nothing you or Lizzie or Shakyamuni Buddha himself can do about it. I'm going to have myself a good pull, and you're going to watch! Self-castration is no answer to the problems of the patriarchy, and I'm tired of feeling guilty for the sex scandal in particular, and for being a white cisgendered middle-aged American male in general—especially considering how little I have done with my privilege. Plus, I'm horny.

I Google "real amateur ebony orgasm" on my laptop and click on a YouPorn link. Suddenly an alternate red screen pops up— someone named Jazmin is preparing to play with herself live. All she needs is my credit card number to make her come. I diminish my main screen, find her. She regards me intensely from her fake bedroom, her lips like rich red pluming gashes, her eyes an electronic tangle of colored contact lenses.

I try to close her window, but my Mac cursor turns into a little spinning ball.

Shit, what's going on, do I have a virus? My Mac Air is thinking.

Don't think, do! Give me female-friendly orgasm porn!

I am one click away from a website that has archived every news item about Roshi's sexual misconduct, for we are a society that will no longer tolerate the abuse of women. Yet in the corner of my screen is an ad featuring a green humanlike creature with rolls of muscle and fat that vibrate and quake with GIF monotony as it pummels a naked cartoon girl one-tenth its size.

We are a schizophrenic culture.

My original click loads. Up pops a black woman whose breasts are cannonballs made out of plastic gel and body hatred. Her vagina is shaved and gleaming, as though sportfucking is an Olympic event. A balding red-faced maniac fucks her from behind with a great and hateful concentration. He closes his eyes and makes a face that is not quite orgasmic; rather, it's as though a painful pressure has been released—like he's farted through his dick. She apparently feels this loving gesture inside of her, her cue to shout-fuck her way to a climax that sounds like she has just lost her balance and is about to fall down a flight of stairs—"AHHH— WHOA. Wha . . . ooooaaaah."

This is not what I had in mind.

I shut my laptop.

Tonight I will have a righteous wank, I will "touch myself" the way leading ladies do in mainstream romantic comedies. I light a stick of incense. It's on, little guy! No porn, no fantasies, just me and you. I'm gonna love on you tonight! I've tried this before. Sometimes it even works. Tonight, though, I feel like a eunuch stroking his phantom penis.

I try to conjure images of ex-girlfriends, but I keep thinking of the husbands who have made them so happy, looking on as I pound the vaginas that delivered those beautiful kids I always see pictures of all over Facebook. No, this will not do. The very act of pleasuring yourself during a sex scandal feels like a violation against the female gender. As Andrea Dworkin said, all sex is rape—even the sex in your head, I suppose.

Never a good sign when Andrea Dworkin shows up in your masturbation fantasy.

I think of Lizzie on the dance floor in her leggings and huge cowboy boots, towering over the small Asian women she so admires, trying to have fun. It chokes me up. What would happen if she came home right now and caught me clutching my little worm and dribbling pre-cum on the silk comforter that she had specially altered to fit Roshi's tiny body?

I'm not jerking off, but I'm not letting go, either. Am I cuddling with my cock? I'm holding it with a certain amount of urgency. Is it a prayer stick? Maybe I should grab one of those new ceramic knives Lizzie can't stop talking about and just cut it off.

I get up and wander into the kitchen.

She is standing there.

Oh God, you're back.

She's come to me recently, in dreams. Sometimes she is someone I've never met, and yet I still know every pore of her skin by heart; once she was the wife of a friend. Sometimes, but not always, it is sexual. We spend hours melting into each other, whispering; very often she tells me something right before I wake up that I can never remember. And when I wake up I always feel incredible, not even loved, but like love itself, like the woman I need is inside of me.

Today she is black-skinned, shining under the kitchen track lighting like a Nigerian goddess. Full-bodied, naked, hands on hips, hair everywhere.

Her eyes shoot from me to the door. Someone is climbing the stairs of Roshi's apartment.

I've fallen asleep on Roshi's bed—I snap awake, pull on my underwear, pull down my robe skirt, lunge for the door, unlock, and open it.

Lucy is standing there.

She has lost so much weight that she looks like a kitten with really long legs. I love this cat so much. I also love the idea of stroking something, anything, other than myself. But I cannot touch her.

"I'm sorry Lucy, but I'm pretty sure I'm allergic to you."

She slowly closes her eyes, then opens them. This is her cat way of screaming in agony from the cancer that is devouring her insides. I lean in close and breathe hot breath on her, as if she were a plant. She points her nose, trying to touch mine. We're almost there when I hear a scream.

I dart around the shoji screen.

Roshi is grimacing.

"*Oshikko*? Pee?" I ask.

He nods.

I push down the back of his leather chair and recline him, pull up his thick cotton skirt, and pull down the front of his gray diaper. As I'm bending over him I see that I have a huge erection under my robes. I reach into his diaper and lift up his scrotum. It is hot and wet, quite lively down there. I yank out the soaked bladder-leakage pad, use my teeth to tear the adhesive tape off a new one, stick it to the inside front of his diaper and pull the diaper back up.

He purses his lips. This means that he's finishing peeing. He does not open his eyes and does not see me moving my face closer and closer to his.

"Roshi, you can't hear me, but there's something I want you to know. I wish you were dead."

There's that ceramic knife Lizzie loves, sitting on the kitchen counter. I use it to quarter a daikon radish. He's so vulnerable. I could pour anything into his G-tube. Using the Vitamix I blend daikon, three crushed garlic pills, a squirt of fish oil, a pitted umeboshi plum, various vitamin powders, and two cups of ionized New Age voodoo water for which a fan of Roshi's paid ninety dollars a bottle. I suck ten milliliters of this nutrient sludge into a plastic syringe.

In my mind Lizzie is telling me that this is not the right combination of ingredients, and I'm telling her that I have my own damn recipe. It's too thick, she says. You're too thick, I counter, pointing to her head, which is my head, which is where she's coming from.

I storm into the living room. Roshi's sitting upright, eyes closed, chin tilted upward, like a hunting dog reading the wind. I reach into his robe and study the smooth braille of his belly until I find his G-tube. I work my fingers up the warped, pebbled plastic to the tube's end, uncap the orange nozzle, and jam the syringe in it.

I try to depress the plunger.

See, the Lizzie in my head says. It's too thick.

Roshi makes a face.

Oh, gimme a break, you can't feel this.

I get about half the gunky liquid through the G-tube and into his stomach when the flow stops. I cannot depress the plunger any further.

I start to sweat. I never sweat. More people are appearing in my head now. Lizzie's right, my mother tells me. You never respected me and now you don't respect her. Don't take her side, I think. She's no better with men than I am with women, and you were no better with me than I was with you.

I can't work with all these people watching me.

I struggle to depress the plunger and force the gunk into his gut, but it's like cement, it won't budge. I've clogged the G-tube before, but never this badly. My head is spinning, my boner is bobbing, and I'm talking openly to myself. Roshi can't hear me because his earphones are on, and he can't see me because his eyes are closed, but he can feel every bit of this. He has that face. His eyebrows, as long as the legs of a crane fly, are bunched, the corners of his lips drawn downward. Orca-sized men in black-cloth diapers, four tits like bulging cartoon eyes, ram their naked bulks into each other on TV, the slap of it coming through Roshi's headphones. He's slumped in his chair with one leg up on the square footstool, headphones cocked sideways as he leans on his hand.

He opens his eyes and stares at me as though properly gauging the situation and finding that it matches his worst expectations. He frowns in a purposely ugly way and closes his eyes.

The voices in my head, every last one of them, scatter. You could hear a pin drop inside me....

My chest buzzes—I am being electrocuted! No, I tucked my cellphone into my robes. Someone's texting me.

"On my way back"

Lizzie! She was supposed to be out all night.

I type "Huh?"

"Ten minutes away"

"Haha no rush! guys night out I mean in ;)"

"Right. Coming back now."

I throw the phone across the room. This is not good. If she sees Roshi like this it'll be last night all over again. . . . Think like her. *Think!* What would she be yelling at me for not doing if she were here right now?

She would already be packing for the hospital.

I start tossing Roshi's dental pic and drool rags and long underwear into a "Leonard Cohen: Old Ideas Tour" tote bag when I remember what Lizzie said back in February when we brought Roshi home from the hospital: *He will not survive another trip there. No way, no how. It'll kill him.*

I kneel down. "I'm sorry, Roshi."

He does not open his eyes. I have never before seen the face he is now making. It appears to be involuntary. There is a pop outside. The LA sky fills with electric explosions, bursts of false blue light. Fireworks have been going off all evening. I have no idea why.

I rush into the kitchen. Last chance. Hail Mary . . .

A clogged G-tube. Can they even put that on the death certificate?

I wash the syringe in the sink, dip it into the Zojirushi hot-water dispenser, suck up ten milliliters of 195-degree water.

Back into the living room.

Roshi looks up at the atomic clock. So do I. Lizzie has a nanny cam, doesn't she, it's in that clock—she caught me on film saying, "I wish you were dead, Roshi." This is senior abuse. I can go to prison for this. I will be raped in the shower. I will have to eat prison ham.

My phone lights up—it is poking out from the dirt of a potted orchid, where I threw it.

"Front door unlocked? Pulling into driveway now."

I stick the syringe into Roshi's G-tube and pinch the rubber valve tight around the tip to hold it in place—I push down on the plunger, my thumb trembling.

Roshi's body jerks. Something's going on inside his stomach.

I press harder, struggling to hold the syringe in place as the pressure from my thumb on the plunger threatens to send it spraying out of the valve.

The clog, the blockage, the motherfucking stuck spot just won't give.

I feel something brush against my bare calves under my robes. I glance down—*Lucy*—I fall back, tugging Roshi's G-tube. He screams. My thumb and index finger slip. The plunger depresses.

Hot water blasts across the front of Roshi's robes as a stream of goop backfires out of the G-tube valve in an explosion of green.

Then I see it lying on the carpet in front of him: a tube of gray flesh. About four inches long, lacquered in blood. Is it an uncircumcised penis? I must have pressed down so hard on the plunger that the pressure caused Roshi's dick to pop right off of his body. I castrated my Zen master.

No, that doesn't sound right. A more plausible and horrifying truth emerges. It is a length of intestine. Somehow I tore out a piece of his stomach through the G-tube hole in his belly.

A voice comes from behind me: *This sangha is full of violent men. And you're one of the worst.*

It is the black woman from my dream. She is standing in the middle of the room, though she is not reflected in the mirror leaning on the bookshelf behind her. Dark, shiny, naked, her great mane haloing her, she points Lizzie's ceramic knife at me.

Please help me, I say.

Help yourself. Face your past.

I don't know how.

Start with the incident in Atlanta.

I don't want to go there.

Go. Just don't stay.

This stuff is so hard to talk about.

Start with Lizzie. What did she say? It's right there in your journal. The words don't lie.

"I want you to see this."

It is dawn. We are in the old airstream trailer in her Mom's backyard. It is a silver tube of tension. Lizzie and Roshi are screaming at each other. The bruised clouds in the southern sky have just burst. Rain clinks the roof and weeps down the windows—

Get to the point.

She leads him, roughly, from the couch to his swivel chair. I am terrified, and a bit annoyed. I really don't want to see this side of my teacher. We have an unspoken agreement. I treat him with the utmost respect, and he keeps human sides like this to himself. He is laugh-shouting, pointing at Lizzie and talking to me through her translation: "This inji's too strong! She'll never find a husband!"

As if speaking to my discomfort, Lizzie flashes her eyes at me: "I want you to see this."

She yells something at him—and that's it.

He grabs her hair and pulls it, snapping her head back.

He laid his hands on her.

That's what I saw. It was put in front of me and now I'm putting it in front of you. It happened quickly—so does this: Lizzie leans into him and shouts "Yeeeeeeessssssss Roshi!"

She is not upset. She is not afraid. Her eyes are bolts of lightning, like an Olympic gymnast the instant she's stuck her landing. And suddenly the air is clearing between them, soft fluid movements as she ties his bib from behind and he pats her arm, and afterward I am a wreck, I want to kill him, you just don't do that, you don't physically abuse your helper, a woman—*anyone,* for that matter—even if she is twice as strong as your geriatric ass. Lizzie takes me outside. The sun is burning a hole through the clouds. We stand under the mossy, dripping shade of a live oak tree.

"You just don't get it, Roshi's from a completely different culture, a different time. Meiji-era Japanese monasteries were not 'safe spaces.' You got your butt whipped! And ya know what? You walked away better for it."

"Roshi just hurt you."

"He *upset* me. There's a big difference."

"He goes too far."

"No, he goes where you need to go."

"If he ever touched me, I'd be out of here."

"Yup. That's why he's so gentle with you."

"Because that's how you *should be* with a student."

"No, because that's *all you can take.* Roshi taught me how to stand up to my ex—*after the fact.* Do you know what that means? *He helped me to heal.* I spent eight years in therapy but I never got anywhere until I met Roshi."

"But are you okay?"

She points to the trailer. "You ever met anyone who showed you more love than that old man?"

"No."

"And yet you draw all these lines in the sand around your relationship with him. That's why you're still stuck. But instead of pushing through, you step back and write about your Zen failures, and you publish, and you get the world to affirm you, and so you never really pass through these deep dark places that you pretend you pass through on the page."

"This is not about me."

"Well if it isn't, that would be a first. Honestly, the best thing that could happen to you is Roshi slapping you upside the head. This practice ain't for wimps."

"That's abuse, not Zen," I shout, but do I really have the right to counter her interpretation of what happened that morning, especially given that she is strong, clear, and healthy enough to be able to speak for herself, but also that *I know where Roshi was coming from*—I've word-slapped her stubborn ass too many times to count, and she's verbally beaten the fuck out of me right back, to the point where I've thought, *My God, it's like I'm having a root canal on my heart without Novocain.*

Like last night?

She wouldn't stop hammering me—*You don't know where you stand!* I called her the C word—yes, that one (*cunt*). She called me the C word—yes, that one (*coward*). I balled up both fists and punched my own head, three quick raps, which sounded like three piles of meat hitting the pavement in rapid succession— for the next four months, every time I open my mouth past a certain point I will feel a sting in both temples. My cunt comment hurt her more than Roshi's hands did that morning in Atlanta, and my own fists hurt me more than her calling me a coward, which pretty much sliced me to the bone, as she knew it would.

So who's the abuser here?

"Shozan!"

Lizzie is standing in the middle of the room. She is reflected in the mirror leaning on the bookshelf behind her. I see the room through her eyes. It doesn't look good.

"What the hell?" she asks.

"I made a mess."

She pushes past me. Her foot twitches midair, as though sentient and sniffing. Beneath it—the blood-oily tube of gray matter.

"What in God's name…?"

"It is the aborted fetus of the patriarchy. I tore it from Roshi's stomach."

She steps over it. "Looks like cat barf to me. Please clean it up."

Roshi closes his eyes and turns his head slightly, as though it is all too much to bear. His favorite sport is not sumo. It is playing two students against each other.

"He's angry," she says.

"Who isn't?" I reply.

Her breath is even, but audible. She's trying to stay cool. You really have to be able to fight with a partner in a compatible way. It's not whether you get along with someone that's important. It's how you don't get along with them that truly matters.

"I clogged his G-tube."

"Again?"

"Yeah. I'm sorry. I already packed for the hospital."

I hold up the tote bag—from the wrong end. Everything spills onto the floor. She takes in the mess all around her. Her resolve firms. It always does in moments like this, whereas mine inevitably softens.

"You hate Roshi," she says.

"I love Roshi! I would have had his baby," I say.

"You're ashamed of him."

"I'm just sorry people were hurt."

"It's like you want to apologize for ever having met him."

"No. I'm done apologizing."

This seems to satisfy her. "Good. Then start cleaning up." She goes to work on Roshi's clogged G-tube with a foot-long pipe cleaner that she produces out of thin air, like Batman pulling a weapon from his utility belt. I fetch a spray bottle of Simple Green. Lucy's cancer barf is unlike regular barf in that it appears to have been heaved into Roshi's room straight through the gates of Hell. Such is its color and stench. On my knees over this thing I feel that it is I who have vomited it up from deep inside me, as though something dark and heavy has passed through my soul this evening. Passing a koan is not like passing a test in school. It's more like passing a kidney stone.

Lizzie plunges hot water through the unclogged G-tube. She jumps up, triumphant. It's been a while since we've held each other's gaze. I got into the life of a monk to avoid the kind of domestic scene that has now become the heart of my life as a monk—arguments with the missus, spoon-feeding our charge, general embarrassment around even the idea of sex with each other. I look at the two of us and I think that we embody all of the problems between men and women that have plagued our sangha, only sometimes I'm not sure who's playing which role.

"How are you?" she asks.

"Okay. How about you? Good time dancing?"

"Yeah it was okay. Loud, so loud. All these young people drinking and smoking pot and looking so cool. I'm like Slender Man around them—tall and faceless."

Light fills the room—the fireworks persist.

"What's going on out there? Is it a holiday or something?" I ask.

"Hell if I know. Can you help me?"

I take Roshi's forearms, pull him to his feet. She whips down his diaper, dapples Aquaphor on his butt wound, pulls up a new diaper. We slide him out of his green-stained robes. I guide him forward, she braces him from behind. He's like a big toddler walking in diapers.

"Yoosh! Yoosh! Yoosh!" he says.

We are almost at his bed. He stops, looks to each of us, touches his forehead to each of ours, speaks. Lizzie translates.

"*You* are my legs. *You* are my legs."

7. The Final Koan

I have been ordered to give Roshi a foot massage. I can hear Lizzie thump-bumping downstairs in the laundry room. Lucy looks up from my lap with yellowing eyes. I stroke her with one hand and rub Roshi's foot with the other. These two dying beings, the patriarch and the pussy, with me in the middle, fighting back a sneeze.

A candle flickers. I study Roshi's face through the shadows and light. I can read anything into it that I want to. We project so much onto our teachers, all our hopes and dreams, and when they fail to live up to our expectations we project all our fears and demons onto them. The one thing we never do is allow them to be human.

It was the humanity of my mentor that got me hooked on Zen practice. I was just beginning to explore Zen as he was just beginning to explore his sexuality, and a lot of his metaphors revolved around gay sex.

"You gotta learn to bottom," he told me.

"Come again?"

"You're an angry young straight white dude, man. You think the world belongs to you, and so you just try and ram your way through it, grabbing whatever you want. You have to learn to take a dick. Otherwise, you'll become a dick." He saw the look on my face. "What I mean is, you gotta open your heart and let the big bad world in."

To his horror, before we went out the next three times I put on a black dress, wig, and heels and transformed myself into . . . what, I still don't know.

"You are the worst drag queen ever," he told me. And I was. "You try walking around in heels all night! It's not easy being a woman!" sassed my inner bitch. I scowled at restaurant employees with my raccoon eyes and smeared lipstick. I even got into a physical altercation with a white guy dressed like Charlie Chan at the WeHo Pride Parade. I remember thinking, *Holy shit, am I going to have to take off my heels and throw down with this racist Charlie Chan?* Dressing like a lady made me act like a grouchy old conservative man.

"I need to find my voice as a woman," I told my mentor.

"You need to learn to listen. There's a true woman somewhere inside you, but you keep speaking over her."

We reached a point in our relationship where I started falling in love with Zen. I needed to know if he was giving me the real thing, or if this was all a ploy to get me into bed. I made it clear what I was after. The only Big D I would bottom for was the Dharma. Fortunately, he didn't use his status as a Zen teacher to try and get into my dress. The teachings existed within him alongside some pretty crude human traits—lust, stubbornness, and an obsession with his weight. But when those teachings came through him, there was nothing he could do to taint them. As Zen Master Hakuin said, "Gold is still gold, even when wrapped in straw." I didn't understand it then and I don't understand it now, but it seems to be the case that the purveyors of truth are not always the purest examples of it. Which I guess means there's hope for all of us.

Back at Roshi's bedside, I stop massaging his feet to see if he will awaken. That face—so ancient, returning to its source, the flesh disappearing into its own softness, laying bare the cradle for what little life he has left: a big hard skull. Watching him lie there is like looking at an ultrasound of death.

Roshi! You are the grand old man of Zen—and you are also a dirty old man who hurt students! How can I make sense of this? I want this story, your life, to come down to something, but it never does. It just keeps opening back up. For the last five years a filmmaker has been shooting you for her documentary—before, during, and after the scandal. What began as the simple tale of a great Zen master has evolved into something far more complex. She has hundreds of hours of footage and no clue how to shape it. We've talked at length about the narrative problems in trying to show both sides of your story. Neither of us has a conclusion. Do you?

I open my laptop and click on a folder of her footage. I want to hear your voice, Roshi. That soft, beautiful cadence. Those words. Your teachings.

I need a hit.

I open a clip and rewind to a time before your first, second, and third deaths. We are pretending to do sanzen together for the camera. You once told me, "To become great monk you must become great actor." The only thing worse than failing a koan is having an audience for it. Lizzie is in the background. Someone is audibly moaning. Is that her? Must be her. Doesn't sound like her. The moaning is pleasurable.

Where is it coming from?

Not from this clip of Roshi . . .

It has to be.

Oh my god. Oh my fuck.

Am I going crazy? I am going crazy. For real this time. I'm hearing voices. They're no longer in my head. They're in the room.

There's someone in the room with me.

Yeah that's right.

I spring to my feet—Lucy spills from my lap. A shadow flashes behind the shoji screen. I run around to the other side to catch it. There's nothing there. Poof—a firework cuts open the night, bright guts spilling into the room. There it is again—a deep haunting moan, now coming from Roshi's bed. I sprint back around the shoji screen. No one there, just Roshi. I study his face very closely. Is he doing this to me?

You're so bad.

My eyes drop to my laptop on the carpet. I minimize the documentary clip with Roshi. I maximize another clip. I have to laugh.

Remember Jazmin, the live-cam girl? I didn't close out of her window earlier. She's been in my computer this whole time, trying to entice potential customers to watch her touch herself. There she is, lips like blood blossoms, kneeling on her fake bed, fixing me with her prismatic eyes.

Another voice—this one Roshi's. I've just failed my koan for the camera.

Completely dissolve your self. I need 100 percent!

Oh yeah, baby, I need it, give it to me.

Your ego too big!

It's so big. Put it in me.

They are both in their own ways getting excited for the cameras. Their voices become indistinguishable. Moaning and shouting. Teaching and tricking. Love and lust. I can't tell them apart.

My koan still. I shut the laptop lid.

11

One and Four

1. I Want to Die

Roshi's been in the hospital for three days, and the American Medical Industrial Complex is going to diagnose him or kill him trying.

The lead doctor will be with us shortly.

"What's that guy's name?" I ask Lizzie.

"He's Turkish. It's something like Baba Ghanoush."

"We can't call him Dr. Baba Ghanoush."

Dr. Baba Ghanoush takes us into the hospital basement. The walls of the elevator shake. Roshi has just choked down a metallic compound of barium sulfate. Now he will attempt to swallow water while being X-rayed standing up. We wear lead aprons. Two husky hairy-armed workers position equipment. Everywhere I turn a hand-sanitizer dispenser begs or threatens me to use it. I surreptitiously sniff my fingers, which smell like me, which can't be good. They lean Roshi against a screen. He trembles while clutching R2-D2 for support, though when I think back now it can't have been R2-D2. Roshi's whole body shakes as he sips from a cup. They get the thing done, rest him on the gurney.

I've been awake for seventy-two hours. I sit down and go black.

I awaken in front of a monitor playing X-ray clips. Someone's kid sister is wearing a lab coat and talking. She is the ear, nose, and throat doctor. Her assistant is even younger. They are both Korean and they are ice.

"I want you to watch this," she says. The ghostly X-rayed flesh around Roshi's skeleton swallows. "Do you see that?" She is talking to us like *we're* the kids. "That's the esophagus. See this here—this is the trachea. When the esophagus opens there are tiny delicate muscles in the throat that are supposed to close the trachea. Okay? That's not happening. Watch."

We watch. Food goes down Roshi's skeleton's windpipe. The skeleton spasms—this is a cough.

"The food sits in his lungs and grows bacteria. We call this aspiration pneumonia," she says.

"How do we fix those throat muscles?" I ask.

"At his age, you don't."

"What do you mean you don't, how can he eat if the food goes down his windpipe every time he swallows?"

"He will never eat orally again."

Dr. Baba Ghanoush starts talking about drilling a hole into Roshi's stomach and threading a food hose into it and it all sounds like perfect nonsense to me.

Something is happening to Lizzie, I can feel her body language changing, and it's causing me to stiffen and prepare. "What about tea?" she says. "He has to be able to take tea. Every morning he has to have tea."

"He cannot have tea anymore," the ENT doctor says.

"But what about in the morning? He's gotta have his tea in the morning." She turns to me. Her lips are slightly parted. She's so tired she's breathing through her mouth. "Right?"

"He cannot ever have tea orally again," the ENT doctor says.

Lizzie rises. I follow her into the hallway. She collapses. She doesn't have any muscle control and I am holding her tall body up. It gets bad for a moment there. I'm worried that she's asphyxiating on her own sobs. Then she comes out of it to ask me, "Are you okay, are you okay?"

"I'm okay. Are you okay?" Once I am certain she's okay, I say, "But I really have to pee." I bow, for some reason, walk down the hall, lock myself in the bathroom, and fucking lose it. I am weeping fireballs. "Keep it together so Lizzie can fall apart," I say to the mirror. "Man up, you little Buddhist bitch!"

Lizzie and I walk behind Roshi as they wheel him back to his room, and we both sob together the whole way. I lean my head on her shoulder and she leans her head on my head.

"No more tea," she says over and over.

Dr. Edelstein begs to differ. His voice over the phone is that of an odd but canny TV detective walking you through a case. "I've been Roshi's doctor for thirty years now. He's never had any trouble swallowing."

"They want to put a pipe into his belly," I say.

"A G-tube? Who does?"

"Dr. Baba Ghanoush."

"I can promise you this—there's no way this Dr. Baba Ghanoush or anyone else is putting a G-tube into Roshi. Bring him to me."

It took tremendous effort, including practically stealing Roshi out of his room at Baba Ghanoush's hospital near the monastery, and driving him an hour west to Cedars Sinai in Beverly Hills Adjacent, where we languished in the ER for five hours before finally getting an audience with Dr. Edelstein, who straightened his Prada glasses and looked up from his iPad long enough to tell us: "So listen, Roshi is having trouble swallowing. He needs a G-tube."

I walked out of the room, to the end of the hall, where I am now having what looks like an argument with a fire extinguisher. Put your mind on the breath, I tell myself. Or a sound. Or the cool breeze on your earlobes. Put it on something, otherwise it doubles back on itself.

We are now in the realm of sickbed politics. Roshi is a powerful figure who has had a profound effect on tens of thousands of people, all of whom, it seems, want to be in his room right now. Lizzie allows one lay monk access: a world-famous singer-songwriter, Roshi's oldest friend; elegant and wise, accoutred in a fedora and a black suit perfectly cut to his frail frame, the great poet takes me aside: "His condition is serious, but not critical."

I repeat this to everyone who calls.

Two days pass. "He hasn't eaten in a week," Lizzie cries. The G-tube department cannot schedule the surgery for yet another day, and so a team of nurses gathers around Roshi to insert a temporary feeding tube through his nose, down his throat, and into his stomach.

"I had this happen to me once," the poet says in his deep, gravelly voice. He moves his chair to the back of the room. "I didn't like it very much."

Roshi is comatose. Like a magic trick—three . . . four . . . five inches of plastic tube disappear into his skull through a nostril. His mouth opens, and this sound comes out. He is honking, like a wild goose being stepped on. A big Guatemalan nurse grabs his jaw. Four hands hold his head in place. The nurse keeps threading the tube deeper and deeper into his gasping face. His eyes are wide. He is screaming from the reptilian part of his brain. What is coming out of his throat is, for me, a single message: *I want to die.*

2. Where Are You?

Roshi returns by ambulance to our LA temple on Valentine's Day. The beautiful nurse waiting in his apartment shows us how to use the automatic pump hanging from the IV tree to feed Osmolite through the G-tube freshly implanted in Roshi's stomach.

There is now a small circle of intimates weighing in on Roshi's health. Some think he'll be dead by summer.

"It's a question of pain management," the home hospice agent tells us in a meeting. She is trying to sell us on her company's services. She turns to the poet, starstruck. "I can't believe it's you."

"I can't believe it's me either," he says.

"What do you mean pain management?" Lizzie growls.

"At this stage in the game we are primarily concerned with making him comfortable. We wouldn't provide him with antibiotics, blood work, or treatments of any kind, for example."

"What would you provide him with?" Lizzie asks.

"Pain relief," the agent says.

"Meaning?"

"Drugs," I say.

"Drugs?"

"Morphine," the agent says.

"No way," Lizzie tells me later. "Hospice is for the dying."

"Lizzie ..."

"He's a Zen master, he's devoted his damn life to having a clear mind. Forget it. The second he takes morphine it's over."

"You don't know that," I say.

"I know Roshi's body."

She is, without a great deal of thought, taking on Western medicine. For years the only drug she's had this centenarian on has been a single children's aspirin a day. Now she's weaning him off the heart medication, diuretics, and whatever they're giving him for his lungs. She shows me the label for one of three antibiotics they put him on at the hospital.

"What's that say?"

"Side effects may include ... *Death*. Wow. It says that like it's no big deal, right next to vaginal discharge."

"Roshi is fine. All these drugs are killing him," she says.

Dr. Edelstein calls. Normally I can feel him frowning through the phone. He frowns even when he is smiling. Sometimes when he is laughing it looks like he is crying. I can tell it's serious because he does not sound like he's frowning. This means he actually is frowning.

"What's going on downstairs?" he asks.

I look at the floor. "Well Fuko is in the kitchen, I think he's boiling turnips—"

"I'm talking about Roshi's *bowel functions*, man, is he able to use the bathroom?"

I relay an incident from earlier this week. We were getting Roshi out of bed when he farted a sad little series of Morse code-like farts. Lizzie disappeared into the bathroom and returned with something a little too large to belong up someone's ass, which was where it was going.

"Sorry Roshi," she said.

In the suppository went. Now Roshi was wide awake, looking into my eyes. Suddenly the shit was flowing. Then he started coughing. A stream of liquid crap ejaculated out of his ass in time with his coughs, spraying in erratic directions as he cough-squirted, cough-squirted. Lizzie grabbed a disposable bed pad and deftly blocked the airborne shit sauce—now spraying here, now there.

"Yeah, well, get used to that. He'll never get his bowel functioning back, not at his age," Dr. Edelstein says. "Is he walking?"

"No."

"How's his mind, is he clear?"

I sigh.

"Mind, legs, bowels. If you've got two out of three, maybe you're okay. One out of three, trouble. Zero out of three? Hospice."

I would rather fight with Dr. Edelstein than Lizzie, so I say, "Hospice means we are legally obligated to believe Roshi will be dead in six months. We don't believe that, legally or otherwise."

"What is it with you Zen people? Listen to me, there is a *100 percent chance* that Roshi will not recover from this illness!"

When I tell Lizzie this she says, "There is a 100 percent chance his head is up his ass."

There are three stages to Roshi's resurrection: spitting, moaning, and talking. It begins with the spitting.

A human being produces two to four pints of saliva daily. It has to go somewhere. For Roshi it goes into Kleenexes. Hundreds of them. He can't swallow, so he spits. Every thirty seconds. All day. Silence comes only when he drifts asleep and drools on the washcloths Lizzie has strategically tucked into the collar of his nightshirt.

Days pass. The spitting increases—once every fifteen seconds. There's a rhythm to it, he's hacking with intent. The flesh around his eyes changes. There is life behind the closed lids. This frightens me. He is getting his energy, but not his mind, back. I kneel by his bedside and stare. There is nobody home except for the spitter.

"Where are you Roshi?"

Lizzie caresses his forehead. "He's just being *it*."

When I enter the room several mornings later, Lizzie is in that same position at his bedside, smiling. I start tearing up. I cry a lot these days, and I lose my temper just as quickly. People think that Zen monks are placid and peaceful, like ducks on a lake. We are also tigers—and Cowardly Lions.

Roshi is feeling the room out with eyes closed, but something else is going on, too. Lizzie keeps smiling. Suddenly I get it. I listen . . . and it lasts.

Silence.

She takes my hand. "No more spitting. He learned how to swallow his saliva again."

The difference between me and Lizzie is that she doesn't think Roshi should be doing better. She is completely with him where he is at. This is inji or caretaker practice.

Unfortunately, Roshi's body is not the biggest problem. Dr. Edelstein visits. Roshi growls, his eyes rolling around in his head like two marbles on a wonky-legged table. Before Dr. Edelstein leaves he gives Lizzie Ritalin pills "to help boost his mental clarity," pills that she throws out, which I fish out of the trash and take, and which do little to boost my mental clarity, though I do clean the room downstairs where I'm staying. You could wash your contact lenses in the toilet bowl it's so clean, but my thinking is pretty much "cloudy with a chance of pain," as usual.

One day Lizzie goes shopping and leaves me alone with our half-starved Zen master. He sits by the window making a bird sound, imitating some lost moment from his youth. Then he goes back to moaning. It has replaced spitting. It is deliberate, primal, and above all, ceaseless.

I learn something about myself as I leave to smoke a cigarette on the porch when I cannot take another second of this subsea mewl of a humpback whale: if I had kids I would, as my father did, have hit them at one point. I have deep compassion for my father as a result, but no compassion for myself, and if you don't take care of yourself when you're taking care of someone else, that's when you burn out and make violent mistakes.

Both my brother and sister worked in nursing homes. They told me how old people die. They die screaming, confused, incontinent. They die while watching *Jeopardy*, spilling Jell-O onto their fronts in an empty room, waiting for visits from the children who will never come. This is how people die. They die in stages, each one worst than the last. *Why did I think Roshi's death would be any different?*

"He's just being *it*," Lizzie says.

"What does that even mean?"

She points to him as he lies in bed at two in the afternoon, smacking his forehead over and over. "It—*it!*"

I watch him being it. *It* is fucking annoying. You have to understand, Roshi is a Zen master to the last, and he is always trying to get under our skin. This is the man, after all, who used to urinate on the bedroom carpet just to see how Lizzie would respond. Sure, he'd blame it on his bladder, which was nearly twice as old as color TV, but she knew better. I used to think she was crazy when she told me these stories, but now I understand. I know that he knows I am watching him, and to my untrained eye there is an undeniably performative aspect to all this moaning and head smacking, like he's going crazy and playacting crazy at the same time.

"It's like he's doing it on purpose," I say.

"I'd say he's doing it *with* purpose," Lizzie says.

As with his spitting, so with his moaning. It intensifies, becomes methodical and mad in equally escalating proportion. And then one morning he turns to me with his eyes wide and it is as though the wave function of his undetermined mental state has collapsed.

"Completely I GRRRRRRRRrrrrrrrrrrrrrrrrr . . ."

"Yes! He is completely in it," Lizzie says.

"In what?"

"Whatever's happening. Good, bad. Doesn't matter."

She groans with him. I groan too. We are the Zombie Acapella Trio.

What is happening right now, in this very moment? Can you do it, and do it completely, so that your thinking mind dissolves into the activity? Can you *do* your life, or will you let it do you? What about your death? Can you do that, too?

There's only one here and now, and you're it.

For Lizzie, Roshi is not fighting for his life or even facing his death. He is manifesting completely in the present moment, which happens to be perched right between life and death. He is turning the simplest activity—first spitting, then moaning, and now talking—into a spiritual ritual through repetition. He is making a religion out of his sickness, and he is dying and being reborn before our eyes.

He repeats simple Buddhist slogans over and over. "One Buddha, one Dharma, nooooo problem." It gets so bad that Lizzie has to shut the kitchen and bathroom doors and sleep on the bathroom floor. She still hears him on a loop out there all night, every night.

"No thinking. No talking. Just Zero!"

At one point he appears to be lucid, so we give him a *Scientific American: Japan Edition*. He tries to read. His face briefly melts, then reforms as panic. "My mind not working!"

Lizzie puts a drop of maple syrup on his tongue. He stops muttering long enough to taste the sweetness. You can see it register on his face. "Completely I . . ." and he moves his mouth, imitating how he just tasted the syrup. Then it goes down his windpipe. He coughs violently.

I know where this is going. "He can't swallow anything but his saliva," I insist.

"Roshi loves food. He needs to eat through his mouth like a normal person. Then he'll come back to us," Lizzie says.

Once a week, Chang, Roshi's speech therapist, goes through the motions of monitoring Roshi's throat. He recommends that if we are going to try and feed Roshi we at least give him Jell-O or pudding. "Mochi pounded rice cakes are literally the worst thing on the planet that you can feed someone with aspiration pneumonia. They're sticky and hard to swallow. Hundreds of perfectly healthy Japanese people choke to death on them every New Year's Eve."

Lizzie feeds one to Roshi anyway. He coughs it back up. Chang takes me aside. "She's pretty strong-willed, huh."

"So is he," I say.

"Look, I've seen a lot of aspiration pneumonias, but never someone this old and this sick. He'll never eat or drink through his mouth again. Got it?"

Lizzie is glaring at us from across the room. "Do you want to tell her that?" I whisper.

Every day since we returned from the hospital, the poet and his assistant have been bringing Lizzie and me healthy gourmet food from LA's finest restaurants. One afternoon they arrive with a greasy bag of Fatburger, a SoCal specialty whose name says it all.

"Let's eat with Roshi," Lizzie says.

Looks are exchanged. We've been avoiding this. It is cruel to dine in front of someone who will never eat again. But she's the boss, so we get plates and napkins and teacups and gather around Roshi, who is busy giving himself semi-coherent three-line instructions on how to live Buddhistically. We sit on the floor around the coffin-shaped coffee table. Roshi's lips are pressed tight and turned downward. Eyes shut. We can all hear each other chewing and swallowing—it's one of those meals.

Halfway through Roshi says "Yah, okay. I also eat."

Lizzie runs into the kitchen and somehow returns moments later with miso soup, white rice, and a pickled umeboshi plum.

Roshi eats the meal.

And we're all crying afterwards.

Days later, Lizzie and I perform our morning rituals, cleaning Roshi with steaming washcloths, brushing his teeth, and taking him to the toilet, which he's started using again. We seat him in his black leather chair. I slide leg warmers up his bony calves; I am startled to find him staring into my eyes, alert, present— watching me. It is finally spring, the scent of jasmine slipping through the window slats. Lizzie opens a box of sweet-bean-filled mochi rice cakes, takes the largest one, puts it before Roshi with a cup of tea.

Roshi takes the mochi, raises it to his lips. And stuffs the whole thing in his mouth.

"Fuck me," I say.

He reaches for his cup, takes a sip, swallows. What happens next, is nothing. He takes another sip.

"Look at Roshi. He's having his morning tea," Lizzie says.

Two months later, hundreds of people watch as I push Roshi in his wheelchair to the lunch tent at an event honoring the fiftieth anniversary of his arrival in America. Lizzie jogs ahead and snaps a picture. I'm looking at it now. There are so many faces I will never see again, people who have died or left our sangha. For one moment, though, we have all come together to honor "the teacher's teacher," as one Buddhist magazine called him.

Only he's no one's teacher anymore. If, as the Diamond Sutra says, the self is truly empty, "like a drop of dew, or a bubble floating in a stream; like a flash of lightning in a summer cloud," then there is no self to be enlightened. There is nothing spiritual to pursue, there is simply day-to-day life, lived to the fullest. The Zen master is gone. I watched him die, and I watched the birth of this weak and wise old man in his place. He used to shout at fifty monks from his high seat in the sutra hall. Now he simply shakes my hand and says, "Good morning. Not *bad* morning, gooood morning!" When I asked Dr. Edelstein how Roshi got his throat and mind back, he said, "There is no rational explanation. Do you Zen people believe in miracles?"

All I know is what I saw: over the past five months, a trickle of life in the bottom of his brain stem became a full human being again. This morning I asked him, "How, Roshi?" He patted my head and laughed: "No true religion without resurrection."

Roshi takes his place at the head table. We spend the rest of the afternoon honoring him through toasts, speeches, and song as he sips sake, yawns, and shakes hands with the young children coming to greet him. We think of aging as a diminishment, but Roshi has not become a lesser version of himself. He's simply dropped his final role. Like all truly old people, he is truly naked. To humbly and totally occupy where you are at in life instead of dreaming about where you could be or chasing after what once was—this is living beyond good and bad, success and failure, life and death. This is Zen.

Four months later the sex scandal breaks.

After Roshi got aspiration pneumonia, I had to let go of my attachment to him as a Zen master. Only then was I able to see what an extraordinary man he was—dynamic and tireless, he taught genius-level Zen at full speed for fifty years.

Then the sex scandal broke and I had to let go of my childish infatuation with Roshi. You can only learn from your teacher up to a point, beyond which his shadow begins to darken your path. So I turned to the practice and principles he'd taught me. They provided guidance and succor when he no longer could.

Then Roshi made it clear he would not name a successor, and the support system for the teachings he gave us collapsed. Our community lost its center, and his main training temples risked becoming a mere collection of properties with no clear leadership or way forward. Chanting every morning to the patriarchs who had passed down our tradition felt like an empty homage to a way of life that my teacher had consciously ended by not naming another patriarch—or, how about it, a first matriarch.

No matter, I thought. I still have the old man himself. He is still with me, drinking tea through his miraculously restored throat and giving small teachings here and there, giving off light.

I can still cling to that, right?

3. The End

Two years later, Roshi is lying on a hospital bed, dying. I'm chewing nicotine lozenges and trying not to be pissed off at Lizzie, who simply thinks—get ready for it—that he is constipated. His oxygen saturation is below 60 percent; the fluid in his right lung has ossified; his mitral valve is regurgitating blood back into his heart.

But yeah. What he really needs is just to take a good dump.

I am in the lobby, trying to be depressed in peace, when Charlie, the lead hospital chaplain, corners me. It is the kind of weirdly synchronistic moment that accompanies death; proximity to the Beyond warps daily reality. As it happens, Charlie has taken Buddhist precepts with the Zen master who moderated our osho meeting after the sex scandal. In the years to come he will teach our community the same council-style practice that she employed so effectively that weekend. Right now, however, he is just a buoyant, bearded, big-bellied guy standing close to me, but at an angle, which transforms what could be a breach of personal space into intimacy.

Words tumble out of me about Lizzie. She wants to be with Roshi the whole way, wants to hold his hand until he is gone, but I'm terrified that some part of her will go with him. She looks more like both an old woman and a stunned child with every passing hour.

Charlie nods and listens, nods and listens. His whole face is an ear—you know how people can do that sometimes? They lean in and their entire skull and the space around it listens?

Then he strikes.

"Let go of him. When you're hanging on, the patient can feel it."

"Do you think we're hanging on?"

"I can feel it out in the hallway before I even come into the room."

When he says this, my whole world turns upside down.

Lizzie leaves me alone with Roshi. We have removed his BiPAP breathing mask. The room is silent save his heaving gasps. He is buried in life-saving equipment; Roshi has begun to look smaller than his circumstances.

I stroke the constellation of needle pricks on his bicep. My fingers love his skin. It is thin and warm, like the belly of my favorite childhood pet, a lizard I named Green Bean. I cradle his head, whisper in a tone I have never used with him before. Our relationship has always been intimate, not personal.

"Roshi, I will take care of the home temple as best I can. I will take care of Lizzie as best I can. It's okay. You can go, Roshi. I love you. You can go."

He opens his eyes and turns to me, and stares and stares. *Thank you, Roshi-sama, thank you. It's so beautiful, you're so beautiful, it's okay, you can go.* We are reading each other's minds, which you can do when neither party is caught up in thought. Tears run down his face. He is crying but expressionless. Later, Lizzie and I will confer: when she said goodbye to him, she saw the same ineffable sorrow in his eyes. His face is a koan, only this time Roshi is giving the answer but we don't know what the question is.

"What about funeral arrangements?" I ask Lizzie. I literally don't know what to do the second after Roshi dies. We've always met him where he was at, but what about when he is no more?

"We don't think about that yet," she snaps. "And it's not time to give him morphine either, so don't even start with that."

"How do you know?"

"I know Roshi's body."

"You're so protective of him."

"Do you know what it's like to be responsible for another person's life? No. You don't even take responsibility for yourself."

"I'm doing the best I can."

"Don't fight in front of Roshi."

"You're the one fighting."

"Shut up. Hand me the clippers."

I catch Roshi's toenails as she snips away.

Roshi's inner circle is now just Lizzie and me, but she and I represent two different sides of that circle. She is concentrated on the last bit of life in him. I see the death that is coming, that is here, and it is taking my breath away.

I gather myself and say, "This is not a private affair."

"What are you talking about now?"

"We can't keep this to ourselves. This is not a private affair. Please don't let him die without anyone but us bearing witness to this."

"You're sick. You want people to watch him the way you do, getting material for your books."

I walk to her side of the bed, put my hand on her shoulder. She stays frozen in her chair. I study Roshi's face. As the eyes of an infant hold life in its purest form, the eyes of this ancient Zen master beam death.

"Can I call the temple and tell them it's okay to visit?" I ask.

They come and go all day. "Roshi is transitioning," I say, leading students and monks from the lobby to his room. I am in my element. "He gave himself to us for fifty-five years and never asked for a thing in return. Now it's our turn. Just sit with him. Two at a time, on the chairs on either side of his bed—hold his hand, breathe deeply, do zazen. Don't cry, don't be emotional, don't make a moment out of it. Just be with him. Give him your presence."

At dusk, Lizzie moves to one side of the room to get Roshi to look at a monk. Roshi's eyes follow her the whole way. Then they close. "That's enough for today," she says.

When everyone is gone, she leans down to Roshi's ear and tells him, through sobs, what the score is. Bad heart, bad lungs, nothing we can do about it. "I'm so sorry Roshi." I record all of this on my iPhone, including Dr. Edelstein saying, "There is a 100 percent chance that Roshi will not leave this hospital alive," which briefly gives Lizzie and I hope that Roshi will leave the hospital alive.

The next morning I awaken on the floor, where I've slept for the past week. The ambulance came for Roshi as we were celebrating the fifty-second anniversary of his arrival in America with the release of his first and only book. A weeklong retreat followed this event, and so it looks like the students who saw Roshi leave for the hospital will get to see him come back home.

You heard that right. The hospital staff has just made explicit what they've been implying for three days: Roshi isn't dying fast enough. He needs to get on with it or give up his bed.

His chest gently rises and falls. He gasped for hours after nurses took off the BiPAP mask, but he seems to have learned how to breathe again using just one lung. Lizzie smiles. "See those eyebrows? Not all gray." We've joked that Roshi won't die until every eyebrow hair turns gray. "Not even close," I say.

He's resurrected once again?! I am not surprised—this is a man who at age 100 was leading a retreat just days after having stents put in his arteries. I pack my dental tape, underwear, and copy of *Infinite*

Jest (which I will probably finish before Roshi dies) into a duffel bag. The sustained self-negation needed to keep another human being alive is draining me. *I love you Roshi, but I can't help but feel like we've come to the end of the story and you're just not playing your part.*

We eat breakfast from see-through containers, compliments of Anastasia, an impeccably dressed Latvian Zen student. I look at my eggs, and my hand through the plastic, holding them. "I need to do some shopping," Lizzie says. "And so this is happening? You're taking him home?" Anastasia asks. She's said her last goodbyes to Roshi three times this past week. She finally got the hang of it the last time. "Looks like it," I say.

Lizzie and Anastasia head across the street to the Beverly Center, where there is a Macy's so deep-bellied in the concrete that cell signals cannot reach you there. They bury themselves in its bowels buying, I think, underwear. Last week Lizzie and I sent out a mass e-mail about Roshi's health wherein we implied: *This is it!* Now I must compose another one that walks that sentiment way back: *Just kidding! We're coming home.*

I pull up Netflix. If I watch *30 Rock* it will inspire me creatively to tackle this e-mail. I stare at Roshi's vitals on the monitor. I fear I have looked at that screen more this week than I have looked at the man to whom it refers. While he, like all humans, is a mystery, the screen, like all screens, tells a limited but verifiable truth that over time becomes impossible to turn away from.

I am tired from the inside of my face down to my feet meat. Roshi's O2 saturation has dropped from 98 to 95. Tina Fey is kind of hot. This, coupled with her sense of humor, makes her very hot, so that I am always imagining scenarios where we tell each other how much we admire each other's work. I wish I had a monitor hooked up to my insides to show me when I'm being cute and when I'm being creepy. This show isn't that good, actually. And I hate the music, which is composed by Tina Fey's husband, who is a very short man and clearly a very supportive partner. I think I'm crushing on Mr. Tina Fey, too.

Ninety-three percent. That's bad.

Yesterday a board member told me that his mother died when he went across the hall to take a leak. "That's what the dying do. They wait for you to leave the room. Then they make a run for the exit." Death, it turns out, is pretty common. Everyone has a story.

Ninety-one percent.

Okay, that's bad.

It's pre-bad, at any rate. When it drops into the eighties that's when I will—it just dropped into the eighties.

I text Lizzie. I call . . .

She's buying underwear at Macy's and can't be reached.

I leave the womb of the room into the bright loud outside in search of the nurse, a sharp-elbowed old white woman who's always looking down at her cell phone. I approach the desk where she is pretending to work. I hate her in T minus four . . . three . . . two . . .

"Can I help you?"

"His oxygen is dropping."

"That'll happen."

"I mean, it's in the eighties."

"Lemme take a look."

That's all she does. Is look.

"Yep. It's in the eighties."

"That's not good."

"It happens."

"What do you mean it happens? It's not good."

She nods. I wait.

"Can we put an oxygen mask on him?" I ask.

She does so, casually mumbles something, leaves the room.

Actually it wasn't mumbled, it was pretty clear, I just can't believe she said it.

Is this woman for real? How unprofessional can you get?

This is weird: Lizzie is never away from cell phone access for this long. How much underwear do you need, lady?

Please answer, please answer, please answer . . .

I sit beside Roshi.

I hold his hand.

I look at his face.

No no, Roshi is struggling, Roshi is struggling, no no—

I storm out of the room.

"Can I help you?"

"YOU," I shout at a big black nurse.

"NOT HER—"

I point to the skinny white nurse.

The white nurse and the black nurse pass a glance between them and the white nurse gets up and starts walking toward Roshi's room.

"NO!"

She keeps going and I'm really loud this time:

"*NO!*"

She stops.

"YOU!" I point to the black nurse.

Then I point to the white nurse: "You said he's *leaving. . . .*"

Who the fuck says that?

Lizzie returns—swings into action. A silver nozzle by the floor, hooked up to a tube on Roshi's oxygen mask—she twists it. The tube stiffens, hisses louder . . . more oxygen reaches Roshi. The black nurse and the white nurse exchange one of their looks. *Yeah bitches*, is what I'm thinking.

We all watch the monitor. Roshi's oxygen rises: 70 . . . 78 . . . 80. The nurses' faces betray nothing save support for Lizzie and me. The white nurse leaves the room. Roshi's oxygen starts to drop.

Time now does a weird thing: a couple of hours pass elsewhere on the planet—in this room, one moment drags itself open for longer and longer. It's hard to describe: it's not just a frown: Roshi's expression is *sinking into itself*. He gasps-gasps-gasps as though drowning in thin air. I can't tell what's going on when I look at him—I can't tell what's going on when I look at the monitor.

"What's going on?" I ask the black nurse.

"Oxygen starvation. Morphine will help with that."

We're here with him on the edge of this moment. He's still in our hands. It takes a unique talent to be able to not make the last choice available to you the instant you realize that it is the last choice available to you, but to instead wait until the true moment for that choice has arrived.

"You're the medical power of attorney, it's your call," I tell Lizzie.

She's looking to the left and to the right, at her invisible options. She's standing at the center of the room, by Roshi's side. She's wearing a black sweater and cowboy boots, and her hair is cut short, and she has on the glasses she bought frames for on her last trip to Japan. This is dragging on and on, and it's all happening too fast.

"He's suffering," Lizzie says.

Roshi is sentient. The room has that feeling still—of his presence. There are students in the lobby waiting to see him. I texted them that we would be bringing Roshi home around noon. Should they be up here now? What are the rules?

"Does morphine help Roshi breathe or does it take away the pain of him not being able to breathe?" I ask.

"It helps with oxygen hunger," the black nurse states.

I've learned to ask: "If it was your loved one, what would you do?"

"I would give him morphine."

"Why?"

"Morphine helps with oxygen starvation."

She sits on the chair with her hands crossed in her lap. In her own way she is as present with Lizzie and me as we are with Roshi.

At 62 . . . 60 . . . 58—his oxygen is free-falling, blood pressure and heart rate shooting up, up, up. I keep having to blow my nose, I have a hospital air-conditioning cold. "He's very sensitive," Lizzie says. "That's the smallest dose we give," the black nurse says. "Half that," Lizzie says. My inner druggie kicks in: "Will that even do anything?"

The nurse is poised with a needle in one hand and Roshi's disconnected IV tube in the other. He is violently exhaling and inhaling, we are down to our last choice. If this is the hardest call she's ever had to make it doesn't show.

"Okay," Lizzie says. "How long will it take?" she asks me.

"About five minutes," I say, having no idea.

The nurse steps back.

Lizzie is on Roshi's right side, where she has been all week, and for the last five years; I'm on his left. She's holding his right hand, I'm holding his left. We are studying Roshi's face, the monitor, our heads seesawing up, down . . .

Everything changes.

Roshi's face goes molten. A wave ripples through it, an inner earthquake. It's like he's been knocked off course. He vibrates, stops, and he's wearing an expression neither Lizzie or I will ever forget. We will debate what it means for years, but not the essential message:

How dare you?

"No no no no no no no no."

"Roshi!"

The next thing I remember is his oxygen—40.

Oh my God we've killed him I'm squeezing his hand *please don't go don't go* searching for his pulse.

His face clenches, almost caving in. Silent roar. *He's losing an organ. Right in front of me.* That stops. Then it happens again, like something's breaking loose inside him. *Gone.* It's like watching someone travel very fast, but he's stock-still, so it's more like something's traveling *from* him. He's taking these great shuddering breaths, I'm waiting for the next breath I'm feeling for his pulse but my hands are shaking I look up at the monitor and there are all these question marks, which blows my skull open.

Question marks? Where's the flat line? The entire monitor is question marks?

I wait for them to do something, to become numbers again. When's that happen, when's that part start?

When do the question marks go away?

When did it happen, when did he die?

I look over at the black nurse, she is calm, and Lizzie and I are kind of screaming.

The clock says 4:25 p.m.

I stand up and start looking around because whatever was in Roshi is *gone*, you can feel it, and the immediate question is: to where? I'm crying and smiling and studying the space above his body up to the ceiling like there is an invisible column of smoke.

"Where are you Roshi?"

We are both touching him. "He's still so warm, so warm."

We are with where he used to be, he's not there anymore—grief is a physical wound, a gunshot, and once the wound closes the dead are gone forever, so you dig it open with your fingers, lunging for them. We take pictures. A lot of them, for some reason. He gets a little more dead each passing second. You can see it in the pictures, like light leaving the sky at dusk.

I descend twelve floors to the lobby and tell the monks and students what has happened: "Let's chant the Heart Sutra."

We enter his room, with us the filmmaker who is shooting a documentary about Roshi. She takes her camera out of its case. Between the ten of us we've chanted this sutra thousands of times before. The gears, however, aren't catching. Suddenly half the room is chanting "Ji Sho Ken Go," and the other "Is Sai Ku Yaku . . ." Our collective voice peters out. The filmmaker looks up from her camera, like, Can I get it from the top? This is so us. We fucked up the Heart Sutra at our teacher's deathbed. The black nurse marches in. "Oh no, uh-uh, you can't be doing that in here, this ain't reality TV." The filmmaker packs her camera. There are no second takes on the deathbed.

Before leaving a nun tells me, "Is Lizzie going to be okay? It's really brutal when they zip up the body in the bag."

"She wants to say goodbye," I say.

Lizzie opens a small black bag, takes out shaving cream and a soft-bristled brush. She fills a pink plastic tub with warm water.

She shaves Roshi's face, his neck, his dead Adam's apple. I lift and hold his head. She shaves the back of it, the front. I pour the stubbly water from the pink plastic basin into the sink. When I return from the bathroom she has toweled off his head and face with a warm wet washcloth. She goes into her toiletries bag and takes out a pair of tweezers.

She gives me a look.

"No way," I say, "You're not going to—"

She starts to.

"Roshi hated having nose hairs," she says, plucking his corpse's nose hairs with her tweezers. She puts the nose hairs from the tweezers onto the back of her hand. Piles them up there, one by one. They're sticking up like little quills. I have to cry in a whole new way after watching this.

She changes his diaper one last time. We take off his hospital gown. His body is stiffening in my arms as I hold him and she slides him into his fluffy white kimono and hakama skirt. She folds his hands at his waist and covers him in a blue blanket. It was knitted by hospital volunteers for his trip home. There is a big red heart crocheted across the front. She slips his golden *rakusu* around his neck, over the heart.

Where are you, Roshi?

4. Wrestling Roshi

Technically he's in the courtyard behind the zendo at our LA temple. His ashes are, anyway. He's surrounded by a rainbow of succulents, black stones, and an asparagus fern that wiggles its thousand fingers in the breeze. Nimbus, our new cat, suns himself on the traditional Japanese Zen master gravestone that marks the spot. Smooth and gray, it weighs over ten thousand pounds and has a distinctive oblong shape, like an eggplant or a thumb's up. In other words, an enormous stone cock marks the spot where my teacher is buried. (Some, and by some I mean me, have also pointed out that it looks like a butt plug.)

Sometimes I sit in silence on the square base upon which this protuberance rests and remember what it was like to practice with a titanic teacher whose legacy is a marbled mixture of dark and light. I don't feel his ghost anywhere on the property. I knew I wouldn't—he was so present when he was alive, I knew that when he died he would never be back. Not that I believe in ghosts, but the cosmos is so far beyond my reckoning that I believe in both nothing, and that anything is possible.

Where are you?

When Roshi first asked me this question in sanzen, the answer was to touch our foreheads together. "Your heart. My heart. Same." I'd been searching for myself all my life. With Zen practice I hoped to finally find something. Burrowing inward on a meditation cushion was some of the hardest work I'd ever done. Then one day it was as though I got to the bottom of my heart, and there was a door, and behind it was my essence, the true me. I turned the handle, but instead of opening inward to some final place, it swung out into a brilliant blue sky. I was staring out the zendo window, completely blown away by the view. There was no me at the bottom of it all. There was a passage to that boundlessness, and the very notion of me was the closed door blocking it.

That night I wrote in my journal, "Instead of trying to figure out how the self is fundamentally empty, think of it like this: You were born from emptiness, and now that emptiness is trying to figure out how to be you. There was never any you there to begin with. Nothingness is attempting somethingness and you are the result. So back off and relax, man. Give it some space!"

And then, just when you start getting the hang of it, the nothing that has become the something that is you, becomes nothing again.

Where are you? This was my first koan, and it will be my last.

One of the last times I met with Roshi for sanzen, he grabbed my forearms and pulled himself out of his chair.

"Roshi what are you doing?!"

"Yah yah—go go!"

With my help he tremble-walked to the window. Then he let go of my forearms. I was so shocked I shouted, "DUDE!" He hadn't stood by himself in three years. He had this expression of wonder and joy—it was about all he could really do in the end, manifest joy as a teaching. He began pointing to things outside the window.

"This is myself! THIS is myself. *This* is myself. All over, myself. Yourself too!"

He spread his arms and reached forward, past the window, the burbling water in the rock garden, the bald head of that fiery mountain man, the sun, setting between two jagged peaks to the west. Then his knees bent and he started falling backward—I grabbed him by the waist under the arms. I was really angry—*What is wrong with you, you could have broken every bone in your body?* I dragged him to his chair and he collapsed.

He went to say something, and then it was like he swerved at the last minute in order to say something else:

"You too attached to this world."

He took my hands and pulled me close and rested his forehead against mine one last time.

"You must completely die with Roshi."

A week later he got sick and stopped teaching.

This was his first death.

When you become obsessed, as I have, with the meaning of life and the question of how to live in this world, you are probably in denial of death. I was. Roshi's four deaths woke me up. First I had to let go of him as my teacher. Then I had to let go of him as the ideal human being. Then I had to let go of the tradition he gave me. At this point something interesting happened. I sat on the cushion without a teacher or an ideal to practice toward or a firm lineage to back me up. All I had was my breath. So I followed it.

The inhale and the exhale are opposites working in harmony to complete each other—like man and woman, birth and death, darkness and light. Together they make up the breath of life. Inhale completely and let what's going on outside of you truly come in. Exhale completely and let what's going on inside of you truly come up. This is Zen practice—not robes, not a teacher, not a tradition. The furthest, darkest corner of the cosmos and the glowing bottom of your heart are on a continuum, flowing into and from each other seamlessly, like the in and out breaths. When you get this in your bones, it's the kind of thing that makes you go to your knees. You realize, as I did, that you don't need to follow anything or anyone except your breath.

Then I saw Roshi take his last breath.

You wait for the next breath to come, you wait . . . you wait . . . that's how you know someone has died, when they stop breathing. In the end even this is taken from you. You cannot attach even to the breath.

Death is with us all along, during every failure, loss, heartbreak, mistake. It's the other side of things, the one we don't want to look at. On a long enough timeline death is the answer to any question we may have about life. And I feel that the same holds true the other way—answers point to questions, death leads to life. They are equal, working together to give rise to and take back this universe.

People always ask me if I believe in life after death. I guess my answer is that I believe in them both at once—life and death are simultaneous, always and forever; there is just one moment, the whole universe, God, playing peekaboo with itself. It's hard to imagine that one day we will just disappear. Maybe it's more like: we are folded back into whence we came. When people ask about death what I think they're really wondering is, Should I be afraid of it? I would say no (even though I am). Whatever is real in us goes on after we die, even if we don't.

But what do I know? When Roshi was dying I spent a lot of

time looking at the monitor he was hooked up to because it had all the answers. Then, at the moment of his death, it started throwing up question marks. Like that monitor, the human mind can only take us so far.

On that note, I said that Roshi hasn't been back since his death, but he visited me once, in a dream the night of his funeral.

I am floating. The ancient city of Athens is in ruins beneath me, Greek columns extruding from smoldering rubble. I descend, somehow less a part of the chaos the closer I get. White people run around with great intensity but no purpose; alone in their calmness are the prostitutes (in fact, there are a lot of hookers, they seem to be running the city).

I float through the open halls of the only structure still standing. There is a great marble block, an altar. On it is Roshi's body. I know exactly what will happen next, I'm floating closer and closer to the corpse and the closer I get the more certain I am that—his eyes open.

He rises up off the stone and for the first time in the dream I have feet and they're touching ground: I am no longer safe.

He reaches for my hands, coming for me like the wrestlers I admired in high school. I played basketball because that's what the cool kids did, but wrestling was the sport for me. I needed to take on someone my own size.

Roshi and I circle each other—are we the same size?

We grab hands, feel the full weight of each other. We are equally matched. He's not exactly naked but he's not exactly not (don't ask me to explain this). I feel that if I let go he will overpower me. He's smiling like he knows something I don't, and we're pushing against each other, cheek-to-cheek, moving sideways, fingers twined . . . dancing? We twirl until my legs have vanished and I'm floating again. We're struggling with or embracing each other, it's not clear when you're this close, and there's tremendous pressure as our foreheads touch, like one of us is sinking into the other, being dissolved—my eyes are open.

Roshi is gone.
I am not sure where I am, either.
Am I awake? In a dream?
Where am I?

Afterword

The Fifth Death

I am in the hunting woods of northern Wisconsin. I am waiting for the shaman. I have a beard and hair—after thirteen years of the Zen monk's life, there is growth atop my head. A big retreat starts today at our LA home temple—*Hanamatsuri*, Buddha's birthday. I should be there. Instead, I've been alone in my father's hunting cabin for over a month.

How did I get here? Where am I going?

Is it spring yet, or still winter? It's all the same once the sun's gone down. The woods around me are cold and black. The mossy log beneath me is wet. A campfire is blazing in front of me. I peer into the dark forest line. The ghost of Leonard Cohen is staring back at me.

"What's the answer?" I ask.

"That all depends on what you want. It's your life, it's for you."

"I'm afraid."

"I can assure you there is nothing and everything to be afraid of."

"That's what I was afraid of."

"If you're courageous, good things come to you. If you're not, you get more of the same."

"How do you know how to make the right decisions?"

"It's easy. Just make them. Then, once it's too late, you know!"

If you stay too long, your cocoon becomes a trap and you begin to rot inside of it. Are my robes a cocoon?

But I can't leave the monk's life, I'm not ready yet. And the home temple still needs me—I promised Roshi on his deathbed I would take care of it. . . .

"Go before they ask you to leave," a monk told me.

The problem started with this book.

Let's put it this way: I showed a draft to Dutch, the big, burly Zen student I wrote about in the scandal chapter. Pretty much the last person I expected to have a problem with my writing, but then that's how it goes. Two months ago we sat down for coffee in LA. He'd put on weight, which made him look taller, redder, and sadder. He folded his glasses and laid them on the table.

"This book, the essay on Roshi and the scandal—it desecrates the dharma."

"Whoa. Easy tiger."

He rattled his coffee cup on its saucer. Slammed it down.

"Desecrates the dharma! As a monk you don't do this, you don't talk about your teacher this way! It will drive people away from the dharma! Do you understand this? People will be afraid to come to Zen centers after reading this."

"It's a hard practice. Maybe I did a public service."

"THIS IS NOT A JOKE!"

That's when what I will call the "public incident" happened. Right there in the coffee shop. The public incident set off a series of events, each worse than the last. Several powerful members of my community became very interested in this book, and not because they like comical Zen essays. Such is life at the home temple. People are always trying to protect Roshi, even, or perhaps especially, now that he's dead. I took a leave of absence from the temple to cut the scandal chapter and write something new. But instead of changing the book, I've begun to think that it's my permanent address that must change.

About that shaman ...

Five years ago I ran into an erstwhile handsome and successful Hollywood friend who was going through a rough patch. He was living in his Toyota Prius and had put on what he called "a whole lot of hate weight." Shortly thereafter he disappeared, only to reemerge a new man six months later. His tits were gone, and so was the hate.

"Where'd you get that body?" I asked him.

"Peru."

He recently invited the shaman he worked with in the Amazon to the Twin Cities, where he now lives. "I wanted him to meet my wife. The guy is amazing. He glows." The shaman and my friend agreed to drive out to my father's hunting cabin to do a special ceremony with me. "It's plant medicine. You need it. Just know: it could get really dark, and there's a lot of barfing."

This is not a casual decision, and I am not doing this for kicks. I need help. "It's healing," my friend said, "but you need to do the diet. You're not taking shrooms in the frat basement. This is a shamanic ritual." One week beforehand: no sex/masturbation, meat, alcohol, oil, dairy, vinegar, avocado, citrus, fish, fatty foods, fizzy drinks, spices, spinach, sugar, yeast, nuts, canned foods, processed foods, tomatoes, marijuana, or caffeine—all of which interact poorly with the industrial strength psychotropic jungle vine I will be ingesting tonight.

"You need to set a clear intention for the ceremony," my friend said. "What do you want from Mother Ayahuasca?"

He insists that the plant has no side effects, but I have noticed at least two very troubling developments since he started doing these ceremonies: a fondness for T-shirts with howling wolves on them, and a tendency to sign off his e-mails with "love and light."

"You've spent thirteen years in a patriarchy, man, a system

where one half of the life principle dominates. This is different. You prepare the ground—that means you do the diet, meditate, and don't have sex or jerk it—Ayahuasca's very jealous, so don't foul the air in that cabin with porn. Then we do the ceremony and you receive the medicine and let the Divine Intelligence work through you. This shit's older than Zen."

"It's older than sitting quietly and breathing?"

The shaman arrives. *Well, that's a disappointment.* He is eleven years younger than me and he is white. He's tall and thin and bearded and ponchoed, like a pot dealer. He's brought a companion. She is younger than him and has long thick legs and sandy blonde hair. The natural resting state of her face is a beatific smile. When you lean in to listen, their voices trail backwards. When you look in their eyes, their eyes narrow and flick away.

The ceremony will take place in my father's cabin. Team shaman immediately gets to work blacking out the windows with blankets and tacking up pictures of Jesus, the Virgin Mary, and a Peruvian *Curandero*, their master. His face looks like a red box with fire pouring out of the eye sockets. There are wooden pipes carved from ayahuasca vines into condors and eagles, old hand-woven blankets, amulets, bottles of rosewater and perfume, half a dozen different tobacco products. They hang seven huge cloth paintings with beautiful, colorful fractal patterns. My father's cabin is starting to look like an Alex Grey painting.

"We will keep these," the male shaman says, leaving my father's gnarled deer antlers on the wall.

"They're the real deal," my friend whispers. "Don't forget to turn off your cell phone."

He and I sit down on our futons. We are given two wool blankets and purge buckets. The underage shamans kneel down before us, about ten feet away. It's time to speak our intentions for the ceremony. I say, "I've been a full time Zen Buddhist monk for thirteen years. But that part of my life may be coming to an end.

The last four, five years have been … they've been rough. My intention is for healing from the past and guidance for the future."

"It was discipline?" the shaman says in his Eastern European accent. "Much strict, Zen?" "Yes," I say. "It's a patriarchy."

We walk up, kneel before him, drink the medicine with Jesus and his mother looking down at us, and a bronze Buddha statue taking the side view. As my friend said, it tastes like "rotten prunes mixed with rancid coffee, cigarette ash, and a good dose of salt." They turn out the lights.

Soon, I feel a twist in my gut, like one of my intestines has gone serpent. The colors on my blanket are moving. The plant starts to fill my bones and veins and I take a step forward, into the experience, instead of away. Big mistake. Ayahuasca is no longer in me—I am in ayahuasca. I grab my bucket, look down into it, and the bottom opens up. It is the Abyss.

Not even Hitler should have to go through this.

This is an experience of Hell.

My mind stretches out over the horizon for infinity. I cannot escape my ego—fear, greed, hatred, madness. The female shaman is moving her eight arms over me. *Thank you thank you* I whisper. She is singing, calling it up, this great cosmic sob is passing through me, coming from the bottom, my face is splitting open but I can't release it. And so it becomes something else. I am turned inside out into my bucket. She whispers to me, "You had good clean purge." That's one way of putting it. Later my friend will tell me, "It was really impressive. I have never even heard someone scream that loud, much less *puke* that loud."

During the evening's single moment of levity, a space-alien-style frog crawls out of my puke bucket. He taunts me with song. "*Old man prostate sittin' in a tree / P-I-S-S-I-N-G.*"

Then:

It is hell it is hell it is hell it is hell. I hear sawing sounds. They are cutting the cord of my conscious mind I can't move I hear slicing and sawing, bloodless surgery. Now the shaman is a black vulture, he's taking the shape of animals and spirits, singing *Medi-cino medicino ayahuasca medicino. . . .* Of their own volition my teeth start ripping out of my skull. Spinal fluid gurgles through the holes. I can't open my mouth it fills liquid is pouring down my throat the female shaman is coughing and gagging over my bucket. She purges. It is like a waterfall into the bucket, but no hint of a human being, no moan or gasp, just this blasting spray of fluid like a fire hose and then silence.

Her face is colorful, painted with self-generating light. "Can I touch stomach?" Her hand hovers over my torso. Then it goes under my blanket. We're about seven hours into the ceremony now. "Your pants down," she says. "Take your pants down. More," she says. "More."

She drives her fingers into my intestines, presses hard, moves some ball, some diamond-knot, around. Just when the pain is unbearable she stops, then she starts again in a new spot. "Your stomach is real mind, true mind." She finishes and flies to her place under the Virgin Mary, and then I hear her sobbing. I gather all my conscious strength because I want this to be a vision, but it's not, it's true, she's sobbing and the reason she's sobbing is because I am a lost cause. I am lost to the hatred within me and she knows it. She tried, but I could give her nothing. He cannot love, I hear her saying. Her voice is beautiful, she sings in Croatian, English, Spanish. *Open open your heart open your heart, trust trust the body. . . .*

I am lying down I look up. I am sinking down. Into a kind of blackness. I am so tired, I have never been so tired, my life force is draining, it's a warmth. I'm in a grave and it's exactly where I belong. I have finally found my place. I am being covered. I am disappearing. Cover me. I don't care anymore. I just want to go. Please let me go. Thank you. Thank you. Goodbye. Goodbye.

The following morning the shamans cook porridge and buck-wheat on my father's gas stove. "She asked you to take your pants down," my friend whispers. "That was so funny!"

"It wasn't like that. I mean, I kind of hoped it would go there, but man, it didn't." After she rubbed my belly and flew away and sobbed, I did get an erection. It was an erection like you wouldn't believe. I think I poked God's eye out and creamed in the socket.

"How are you?" the female shaman asks.

My body is very calm. "It's like I'm uploading the new software."

"Ha ha ha ha. I felt your purging. You were getting up some very, very old things." She has a face like old Croatian land, her eyes tiny pools of blue. She smiles in waves and the land moves. "I feel you were very tight at the monastery. I feel you worry about what the others think and you become tight and try harder and harder but don't feel. It goes back to your father. And his father. And his father. And you brought your father and his father and his father to the monastery with you. And you tried to be man-monk. But you stopped feeling. Now you feel again. The plant, the Mother, says, 'Now you feel again.'"

"You told me, 'You get the trip you need.' Why did I need to go to Hell?"

"*Because that's how you bring the fire back!*" She points to a lit candle. "Now this fire is inside you—here." She points to my belly. "It's okay to look up to other teachers, but you're equally valid to anyone else. You become your own maestro. Your own teacher. Your body, your mind. These are your temple now."

I always wanted to be a great writer. A great thinker. A great monk. A great goddamned something. Ayahuasca simply showed me in Technicolor what Zen has been showing me all along. That I'm nobody. I'm free of a fixed, solid self. Attach to some idea that you need to be, or are, this or that, and suffering begins. Hell is ultimate suffering, ultimate self-absorption.

Hell is interesting, too. That's why I keep going there. In my practice. In my writing. In my personal life. But it's a dead end. Nothing comes from suffering but more suffering. It is not generative. It is an infinite regression. It is the opposite of feeling. All you need is a spark, you don't need the inferno.

I need a woman. I saw that last night. And I need to be my own man again. Self-consciousness has always been my default. Now I want to lose myself in others. The only direction to go is in and through yourself, and back out into the world again. "Making relationship," Roshi called it. You don't need to be great. You need to be complete. You can be complete whether you are working a shitty job at Walmart or you are a world-famous writer. Just walk the path of True Love. When you grapple with life's deepest problems openly and honestly, the ego melts. It dies. There is no such thing as a fixed state of happiness. We face challenges, and in order to pass through them we must die a little, or a lot, and be reborn. This rebirth is the opposite of what one feels during a suicidal moment. It is love of, reverence for, life. It is the pith of all religious feeling.

I want to share this insight, and the practice that leads to it, with others. I want to be a Zen teacher, not just a Zen student or a middle-way manager, and I can't do this at the home temple. It belongs to my teacher, the Roshi, and his legacy, and it always will. This is how it should be. You can't make another man's temple your own.

I need to move out of my Dharma Dad's basement.

Instead of writing a new chapter for this book, I write my resignation letter from the home temple. I explain that as a priest in Roshi's lineage it is time for me to start my own temple, focus on writing, and get some kind of a personal life going. They are the hardest words I will ever put down on paper. But I've made the right decision. You know it's time to move on when you're putting more energy into fighting with yourself and others than you're putting into creating something new. Roshi once said that it's okay to get divorced when you can no longer give yourself to your spouse. This is how I feel about my relationship with the home temple.

The shamans left behind a few *Mapacho*, or filterless ceremony cigarettes that you don't inhale. I light one outside and puff on it. I sit down in the dew-twinkling grass. The birds are going nuts. Butterflies. It's definitely spring. These big fat jetliner crows swooping through insect clouds. Bushy wisps of floating fox fur. I can feel the whole damn forest. I can feel my father back home, the green in the leaves, my own beating heart. There was a fire in these woods a few years back. The place looked like a post-apocalyptic wasteland. Charred saplings reached out of the black earth like severed limbs. The fire cleared the way for new growth. Today the forest is a pulsating paradise of green.

I read a lot of Elisabeth Kübler-Ross when Roshi was dying. She talks about the five stages of grief: denial, anger, bargaining, depression, and acceptance. I think there is a sixth stage, which also signals the end of grief. It is renewal.

I'm forty-four years old and I'm starting completely over. I don't know where or how I will live. I have a speck of money and no plan. I have no home, girlfriend, job, kids, or car. I don't even own a proper belt. Am I terrified or euphoric? I want to remember this feeling. Everything is possible. Everything is possible, and something will happen. I will buy a belt. My new life will begin, step by step. This time around I will not think so much. I will kiss first and ask questions later.

Maybe I'll write *Eat, Pray, Love* meets *Fear and Loathing in Las Vegas*: after breaking up with Zen, our hero odysseys to the Amazon for an ayahuascan holiday in *Eat, Trip, Barf*.

Holy shit! I'm leaving the monk's life! And I didn't even get enlightened.

It's worth remembering that in the classic texts, no Zen master ever hits satori on the cushion. He's always off the monastery grounds completely when he hears the crow cawing or a stone striking bamboo and he suddenly realizes: *Holy Moses! That's what it's all about!* The only place a spiritual practice belongs is out in the real world.

But the real world is a scary place. And it's getting scarier. Do

I really want to go back out there? We are headed for dark times. War, famine, environmental destruction. At some point the human race will have eaten itself out of house and home. It will have eaten the earth, the sky, and everything in between. All that will be left will be for it to eat itself. This is how the human race ends. Just as it began. Hungry.

Where is Buddha then?

Where are you, Roshi?

Where are you?

The first koan, and the last.

Old age, sickness, and death. Our lot, as individuals and a species. If everyone will one day be no one, then we are only temporarily separated right now. Our true home is no home, together. The Zen master Rinzai said, "Before brightness is manifest, darkness is bright." Everything contains its opposite. Nothing exists apart from anything else.

"Beyond right and wrong there is a field," the poet Rumi wrote. "I'll meet you there."

Perhaps I'll buy an old Subaru Forester and travel around the country. There is a wisdom from ages past that runs through the human race straight down into your spinal cord. I will find it on the road, visiting different dharma centers, taking psychedelic mushrooms in the forest, and spending what little money I have on camping gear and Rogaine. When I'm exhausted I'll settle down, grow some love handles, maybe get married. One night I'll lie with my wife and three hundred nights later, our child will be lying in that same bed between us.

That would be a nice ending to this story, which has yet to be written. I look into the child's eyes and I see the future, and suddenly the future doesn't look so bad. Our eyes close, our foreheads touch, and we manifest True Love.

Then we move on to the next koan together.